WHAT IF YOU'RE RIGHT?

WHAT IF YOU'RE RIGHT?

Discover How Right You Are in a World
that Makes You Feel So Wrong

DR. EMILY COLWELL

atmosphere press

To my five-year-old self,
for helping me to uncover all the rightness
that's lived in my being from the start.

"And the day came when the risk to remain tight in a bud was more painful than the risk it took to blossom."

– Anais Nin

TABLE OF CONTENTS

INTRODUCTION

Anxiety owned my life for forty years.

You know what else owned me? My lens of wrongness.

For too long, so many of us have only been able to see everything that's wrong in our lives. What if it turns out rightness is one micro-moment away? It's been perched inside us all along, waiting for us to come home. *What If You're Right? Discover How Right You Are in a World That Makes You Feel So Wrong* is the book that shows us how to end the exhaustion and find we are utterly wise, mighty, held, and whole.

The lens of wrongness is everywhere in our culture. The lens of wrongness convinced me that my anxiety and many other aspects of me were innately wrong and that the solutions lay outside me. This is the case for so many who simply feel the exhaustion of trying to figure it out. This leads many to seek self-help books in an attempt to find relief. They find a book that seems to hold the solutions, so they tackle the steps in the book, feeling empowered and excited to right the wrongs in themselves and their lives. They unknowingly set the intention to master the steps in the book perfectly, so they can finally fix themselves and their lives, and really start living. But before long, life happens, and they fall away from their daily practices and the time commitment this self-care requires. This fills them with self-loathing yet again, for not maintaining their self-care, which sweeps them right back into their lens of wrongness and all the ways they aren't up to snuff. And this is exactly why *What If You're Right?* offers a different experience to all the exhausted women who are buried deep inside their lens of wrongness.

By the time I graduated from Columbia University School

of Social Work in 1994 with my master's degree, I was buried deep inside my own lens of wrongness. I'd already navigated chronic illness for three and a half years, and this illness would go on to persist for another five years. At the time, the doctors didn't yet have a name for my illness, but it involved debilitating fatigue and a slew of other complex, life-altering symptoms. I didn't let any of that stop me, though, as I dragged myself forward, convinced that my body was betraying me. I repeatedly attempted to disregard my body's cues, only to have the cues grow louder. I relentlessly searched for ways to right the wrongs of my body.

At first, I went the conventional medical route, trusting these doctors would know the answers. Yet the answers to my failing health remained a mystery to these specialists, so I turned to holistic medicine out of desperation. This slowly opened me to new perspectives and a deeper understanding of the ways the body, mind, spirit, and emotions are all intricately woven together and impact one another. Slowly, but surely, my eight-year battle with chronic illness improved with the help of holistic medicine and I went on with life.

I practiced as a clinical social worker for ten years, working with homeless youth and their families, the elderly, veterans with schizophrenia, and complex medical and oncology patients in outpatient and inpatient hospital settings. However, my interest in natural medicine only increased during that time as many of those years coincided with navigating what was eventually diagnosed as chronic fatigue and immune dysfunction syndrome (CFIDS). This ultimately led me to return to school to earn my doctorate in naturopathic medicine from Bastyr University in Seattle, Washington. After completing medical school and a residency in family medicine, I practiced as a primary care physician. I unwittingly applied my lens of wrongness to my patients during those early years, frequently joining them in viewing their anxiety, illness, or other symptoms as concretely wrong and needing fixing.

This is what the lens of wrongness does. It pushes us to search for the answers as if we are perpetual self-improvement projects, always striving to fix the parts of us that feel wrong or broken. Only when we do this can we comfortably return home to our bodies and selves and finally start living. The tricky part about this mission to fix the wrongness is that it requires us to go to war against our unwanted emotions or health challenges. Yet these unwelcome experiences occur inside us, which means we are perpetually at war with ourselves and endlessly looking for ways to escape from our bodies, uncomfortable emotions, and experiences.

This perpetual inner war engages our fight-or-flight stress response. When the nervous system shifts into a chronic fight-or-flight response, this decreases immune function and creates a notably higher risk of developing chronic illness. This is exactly what resulted for me as I moved through those eight years battling CFIDS in my twenties. Because my lens of wrongness was firmly intact, my CFIDS joined the ranks of enemy status and I went to war against it, looking for ways to escape from my body that felt so wrong. I've witnessed thousands of my patients experience this along their journeys too.

Something unexpected happened when I began to recognize and understand the impact of my own lens of wrongness on my life and health. I learned to pause my fight against the parts of me that felt so wrong and instead turn *toward* my anxiety, other uncomfortable emotions, experiences, or physical symptoms with curiosity instead of trying to get away from them. I discovered how frequently these unwanted, seemingly wrong aspects of my life turned out to be messengers, offering guidance and wisdom. And I found they'd been trying to call me back home to myself all along, where, it turns out, relief and healing become so much more possible.

For the first twelve years as a practicing physician, I focused on addressing patients' physical health while concurrently tending to their emotional health. But as my understanding of the lens of wrongness deepened, so did the ways in which I realized I could help others find healing. This awareness expanded to my wife, who is also a naturopathic doctor. We've shared a medical practice together for fourteen years and our practice has evolved, as has our understanding of the lens of wrongness. As a result, we shifted the way we help our patients to better reflect this evolution. We created programs that enable us to take patients through a process that explores their physical *and* emotional health and how these two impact one another. She addresses their physical wellness and I address their emotional wellness. We've discovered how uncommon it is for healthcare practices to simultaneously tend to both the physical *and* emotional wellness of their patients in this way. We mentor our patients as they learn how to come back home to their physical bodies and emotions. They come to see all the ways their bodies and emotions have been trying to get their attention by using unwelcome symptoms and feelings. Yet our culture teaches us to disregard these messages and make them wrong. These symptoms grow louder, not because our bodies are trying to betray us, but because they are working hard to call us back home, where they know healing is most possible.

Many of our patients have navigated endless years of chronic health challenges, anxiety, or other emotional health difficulties that have not responded to or only responded briefly to treatment. Yet when they learn to shift from their lens of wrongness into curiosity as they navigate their physical and emotional health, they experience radical changes in their wellness and lives.

When I discovered my lens of wrongness, I initially felt convinced I needed to eradicate it from my life. And many of my patients feel this way too. But it turns out that's not really possible because we're these imperfect humans and a lens of wrongness is cultivated in us everywhere we look! Yet shifting away from using a lens of wrongness in a complete and final way isn't one bit necessary to experience the benefits of this shift when done in the micro-moment.

There's a reason I couldn't help but birth this book. I've learned how possible it is to have a different experience with just about *anything* in our lives when we shift the lens we're using to one that invites curiosity instead of automatic wrongness in the micro-moment. This shift naturally invites us to come back home inside ourselves with this curiosity. It enables us to drop from our relentlessly spinning minds into our bodies and notice what *is* in this moment. And this leads us to discover just how right we've always been in a world that's made us feel so wrong.

What If You're Right will show you that it's *never* been necessary to master self-care tools perfectly to reap the benefits. It will show the micro-moment is our ally, as is learning how to shift in that micro-moment away from the lens of wrongness and into momentary curiosity. Then it becomes possible for our relationship with our unwanted emotions, health challenges, or experiences to transform and open us to the relief we've wanted but always looked for in all the wrong places. I can't wait to show you just how true this can be in many different areas of our lives; so, kick back, read on, and enjoy the micro-moments along the way!

Chapter One

I HAD A LOVE AFFAIR ... WITH MY CANCEROUS THYROID

"You have thyroid cancer, and the biopsy results suggest a 95 percent chance it's aggressive."

That's the call I received from my endocrinologist in December 2017. I was shocked. I'd had biopsies of my thyroid nodules in the past simply because they were present, shown to be a specific size, and my mom had had thyroid cancer years earlier. The needle biopsy procedures were never a favorite for me, but they were certainly manageable. I went for yearly checkups, and everything always checked out, including biopsies. When I went for my routine checkup in 2017, my doctor asked the same questions I'd heard every year, but one question made me pause: Was I experiencing any changes in swallowing?

I had been struggling with swallowing on the right side of my neck for at least eight months. Whenever I swallowed pills, it felt like they were stuck in my throat partway down the right side. It also happened when I swallowed certain foods. Here I was, a doctor, yet I'd never paused to wonder about it. I simply joked about it with my wife, frequently laughing about menopause and how symptoms even climb up into the throat. My body was changing in many ways as I navigated my way through my newer menopausal symptoms, and my mind simply brushed it off as just another one. I mentioned all this to my doc, which prompted his request for a repeat ultrasound, which led to another biopsy. While the ultrasound showed a new nodule more sizable than the others, I continued to feel relaxed about it as my thyroid had never given me any trouble other than having nodules hanging out on it.

Then I got the call. It was malignant and probably aggressive. By the time I hung up, I was trembling violently. The trembling lasted for a solid two hours. No matter how many sweaters, jackets, or blankets I wrapped around me, I couldn't warm up as I sat on the couch trying to make sense of this news. My first thoughts were, "How is this even possible? I've learned to take such good care of myself. I've done so much therapy over the years. I've processed the wazoo out of my traumas. I generally have a positive outlook."

That's when I realized: I'd come to believe that taking care of myself, working through my traumas, and trying to fix myself like I was some kind of perpetual self-improvement project would somehow make me immune to cancer or other unwanted experiences. This thought, of course, led me to the next thought, which was, "Somehow, this must be my fault. I must not have worked hard enough to heal my issues. I must have overlooked something." I felt surprisingly ashamed, as if I'd done something wrong that resulted in this, which only compounded my experience as I sat there shaking violently.

If I had cancer, I must be wrong. My mind had automatically shifted into using a lens of wrongness to view my situation, only able to notice everything awful about it. It kicked into future-tripping as it spun out worst-case scenarios. My daughters were three and seven years old, and my wife and I had been together for ten years. I'd spent time envisioning how unbearable it would be to lose any of them, but I hadn't previously allowed myself to consider what it might be like if I had to leave them too soon. See? Worst-case scenarios from the get-go. As these thoughts highjacked my mind, the powerlessness catapulted me back to that time in my life many years earlier when I was chronically ill for eight years in my twenties. I felt a deep dread as this vortex of powerlessness that had once swirled through my life began to overtake me.

Suddenly, it shifted. As I sat trembling on my couch, I started to feel a strange and overwhelming appreciation for my thyroid. I was stunned to recognize that my sweet little thyroid had been doing *amazing* things to support my body since I was in the womb, yet I'd never once thought to appreciate her! Soon after, I knew I needed to give her a Thywell (thyroid farewell) Party. My sweet thyroid spent almost forty-nine years underappreciated (well, practically ignored) yet remained committed to doing a stellar job of thyroiding my body. Clearly, it was time to throw her a party and flood her with appreciation before she headed out. I shared with friends and colleagues and posted on social media, letting people know that my thyroid would accept letters and notes of appreciation from all those eager to recognize a job well done. This appreciation only grew through this experience and quickly evolved into an all-out love affair with my cancerous thyroid.

As I sat digesting the gravity of my new diagnosis, I became acutely aware of how I *did not* want to feel. I did not want this deep sense of powerlessness. Three hours in, another unexpected question broke through: How *did* I want to feel? Simply asking myself this question felt empowering.

Here's what I realized: I wanted to have 100 percent clarity about which treatments I'd use to address my cancer. I wanted to feel empowered through the process. For the first time in hours, I felt a glimmer of relief. Yet my mind continued to draw me back to a focus on how I *did not* want to feel. Each time I caught this, I shifted my focus to what I *did* want to feel: clarity and empowerment.

Over the following weeks, I noticed that the faster I shifted my focus back to how I wanted to feel as I moved through my experience, the more relief I felt. I repeatedly let go of how I wanted things to look or turn out and instead focused on how I wanted to feel as I moved through it. I reminded myself that I did not have to know how, where, or when the clarity and empowerment would show up. All I needed to know was that's what I wanted to feel no matter what turn my cancer took. Little by little, it came from various places until, one day, I felt 100 percent clear about my next steps. Now I had a tool that enabled me to step back into moments of empowerment and relief when I needed them.

A couple of weeks after my diagnosis, I went to the gym before any treatment had been implemented. As I started my workout, I quickly felt like I was pushing a boulder up a mountain. I had no energy and felt ready to throw in the towel and head home. My mind immediately chastised me, saying, "Oh, great. Look what's happening. You're already identifying too much with your cancer, and now you don't even have the energy to exercise." No sooner had I thought this when I heard a crystal-clear voice say, "Emily, health is pouring through you right now. It's just pouring through you, honey." Looking around with surprise, I quickly realized this wasn't the voice of someone nearby, but was a voice from within. There I was with what I understood to be an aggressive form of thyroid cancer, yet health was pouring through me at the same time, with millions of other things in my body working spectacularly well. And I was simultaneously experiencing a love affair with my cancerous thyroid. Experiencing this rightness changed how I experienced the wrongness of my cancer. I understood how possible it is to have a different experience with just about anything in our lives when we shift the lens we use to one that invites curiosity instead of automatic wrongness. Because let's face it, it's pretty darn easy to view cancer as definitively wrong.

Soon after, I learned strep throat was the culprit in my exhaustion at the gym that day. Ooooh eeeeeeh, you should have seen how *mad* and panicked I was about this! I'd been all scheduled for my Thywell party and thyroidectomy surgery. Then a bacterial infection came along and started to settle into me. I shouted, "Noooo, I have a plan, and I'm sticking to it!" I spent the day fighting it like it was my job. Fighting my strep throat and the potential change in the timing of things. But when I awoke the following day, I felt compelled to shift my focus from what I didn't want to happen to how I did want to feel at the party for my sweet T, and as I headed into surgery. That immediately made things clear again. I wanted to feel excited to wholeheartedly be able to engage with people at the party as we showered my thyroid with appreciation. And I wanted to feel strong as I rolled into that OR. So, I changed the timing of things and postponed my Thywell party and surgery.

I was reminded that timing has wisdom wrapped up in it, even when we can't always see it at the moment. Did I know how the new timing would end up being perfect? Nope. I didn't. I trusted that perhaps I would come to know or not need to know. I was reminded that when I let go of exactly how I wanted those next weeks to look and instead asked myself how I wanted to feel as I moved through this time, relief came over me, and clarity poured in. And that was worth letting go of the timing.

Dance with My Cancer Cells?

After feeling under the weather for a week with a whopping case of strep, it was a joy to feel better. I was hopping around the house doing stuff on my to-do list, which always makes me feel accomplished. The music was blasting, and I was jamming between dishes and laundry. An unexpected desire abruptly descended over me. I felt moved to dance with my cancer cells. I know, it seemed crazy and certainly not something that had ever even occurred to me before, yet it occurred to me that day, so I went with it. I'd already been jamming to the music, but I started to do it with my cancer cells in my mind. I decided to expose them to the joy and appreciation I felt that morning. Well, it was the most beautiful experience. It filled me right up in a way I wasn't expecting and brought sweet tears to my eyes.

An understanding crept into my mind as I danced with those cells: cancer cells are simply confused cells. That's literally what they are. They become confused and start growing in a confused way for that area of the body. And confusion is a state in which I'd spent so much time in my life. Of course, my body created some confused cells. Confusion was a dreadfully uncomfortable feeling for me in the past and was often closely tied to fear. Whenever it showed up, my initial response was to do whatever it took to get it to go away as fast as possible. I mean, who wants to feel confusion and fear? I was always hell-bent on figuring out what was behind it to make it go away. I worked harder and harder to understand it, going over and over the stories it involved. This usually resulted in me feeling more confused, powerless, and freaked out. Not exactly the outcome I was hoping for.

I had spent so much of my life making confusion and fear wrong. I only knew how to use a lens of wrongness to view them. But in the few years leading up to my cancer, I'd played with not making confusion and fear (and even my anxiety) wrong but simply allowing the feelings without trying to understand them. It felt foreign when I first began this practice, but as time passed, I discovered how powerful this shift was. Sure enough, each time I applied this shift to acceptance, my confusion and fear decreased much faster, and I moved into more ease.

There I was, dancing with my cancer cells in the family room, when I realized those cells were not wrong. They were simply confused. Now it wasn't about frantically trying to make them go away but allowing them their confusion. As I moved forward in my cancer experience, I talked sweetly to my confused cancer cells. I told them I was there with them and that it was OK for them to feel whatever they felt. I let go of any of the stories about why the confusion and fear were showing up. It turned out it was a gift that I had developed strep throat the week before because it led me to postpone my Thywell party and the surgery. It meant I had more time to dance with my cancer cells and softly allow their confusion. Now I was left to wonder what this might bring.

DARK NIGHT

On the eve of my Thywell party, I was thrust into a dark night of the soul. Feelings of terror, grief, confusion, and sadness overwhelmed me, and I felt like I might not survive their depth. My mind kept searching to identify the specific stories to attach to the feelings and explain them. I cried many tears. I noticed where I felt the feelings in my body. I whispered soothingly to the part of me that was so scared and gently told myself over and over that I could feel the feelings, that it was OK to be feeling them, and that I was showing up for them and acknowledging them.

Here's the thing about the stories we have. They aren't wrong. Not one bit. We need to have stories that help explain how we feel. Yet I've discovered that how I focus on the stories influences how I move through the feelings. There's often a pull to focus on the stories because it distracts me from experiencing the feelings underneath them.

I moved through this dark night of the soul, doing this human dance of feelings and worried that it would impact my experience at my Thywell party that night. And it did impact my party, but not in the way I expected. When I awoke in the morning, I remembered that it's possible to feel more than one feeling simultaneously. I made room for joy and appreciation to exist alongside sadness and fear. I made room for the stories and feelings to coexist. I wandered through the day making space for all of these emotions to be present until I began to notice a feeling of appreciation FROM the confusion, fear, and sadness. It was as if they had been waiting to be acknowledged and allowed and not made wrong for all these years … and it was finally happening. My feelings gave me a gift by showing up, and I gave them the gift of acknowledgment in return.

When my Thywell party started, I was filled with joy and gratitude. So many wonderful people showed up to celebrate my sweet thyroid and share their love with my family and me. I connected in meaningful ways with so many who attended. The entire house was laden with butterflies (the thyroid is shaped like a butterfly, and she was about to fly away). Polaroid pictures were taken of everyone who attended the party as they walked in and then clipped to a string of lights in the kitchen to remind me of all those who so openly showed up to give me and my thyroid such beautiful love. And to top it all off, my thyroid won a Lifetime Achievement Award from the "president of the American Thyroid Association"! Her heart just filled with joy to receive such lovely recognition.

Two days later, I headed into surgery. I was so tenderly aware of the transformative power of acknowledgment and curiosity about how unwanted experiences may be right, even when they seem so wrong at first glance. My appreciation of my thyroid and acknowledgment of all she'd done for me for the last forty-nine years changed my thyroid cancer experience. It made it possible for me not to make her cancer wrong, which I honestly hadn't known was possible. My acknowledgment of some unbelievably uncomfortable feelings that showed up through this and my curiosity about how these feelings might be right instead of wrong led to an expansion

I couldn't have imagined. YES, on the cusp of my sweet thyroid's departure, I thanked my cancer for these beautiful gifts I received.

POST-CANCER CURVEBALLS

After surgery, it was a different story. Transitioning to life without my physical thyroid was more challenging than expected. It felt like I had a postpartum brain. My memory was gone, accompanied by a fog that resulted in numerous, repetitive conversations with others because I had no idea I'd already talked with them about it. It was a real trip for me ... and perhaps for those who embraced those repeat conversations too. Depression was also a big part of the picture. Oy, the depression. When the body doesn't have enough thyroid hormone, depression is a typical result. And depression descended upon me during that time. I fought it like a champ. I made my depression *so* wrong. I felt embarrassed that I was depressed. I didn't want to be depressed. I'd felt so much better *with* cancer than I did without it. Then I discovered another story: I believed I was worth less in my depressed state than in my high-vibe form.

Depression is an experience with which I am familiar. It had been a good ten years since I'd last swum in those waters in any significant way, but those waters I knew. But this time, I'd shifted my lens from wrongness to curiosity. It was interesting to experience it again with a different lens. I understood the power of my focus in an updated way. I understood the power of the stories I tell myself too. During those months of depression, I witnessed my mind spinning tales. Those convincing tales were so familiar because many of them showed up every time I experienced depression: I didn't feel understood, I felt forgotten, and I didn't feel loved. Those same thoughts showed up this time, too, yet I could sometimes recognize that they were stories, which automatically invited some ease into those months of depression through which I waded.

Interestingly, in the last week or two *before* surgery, I'd begun to notice that the swallowing difficulties I'd experienced for eight or more months were still present but diminished. After surgery, I was stunned to learn that the mass the surgeon found was three times smaller than at the time of my diagnosis. While numerous factors pointed to a more aggressive type of thyroid cancer, the pathology report showed the most unaggressive type possible. I can't begin to explain all of this, but this experience changed something for me. It made me understand more deeply just how powerful it is when we come home to our bodies and emotions in each present moment. I discovered that even the things that appear the most wrong in our lives can ultimately hold unexpected gifts for us.

Did I completely learn this and live this way ever after? Nope, I needed to be reminded eight months later as I struggled to balance the new thyroid hormones that my life now depended on. I'd never been on thyroid hormones before and finding a combo and dose that allowed me to feel how I'd felt before my cancer turned out to be tricky. My energy was nonexistent. My brain struggled to think. My memory was all but gone. I went to work each week, gathering whatever little energy I had to meet with my patients. Not a day went by that I didn't experience angst over this struggle. My mind was obsessed with finding the solutions and figuring out the correct thyroid hormone dose so I could feel like myself again. You may be familiar with this state of mind yourself. The more you focus on the unwanted situation in your life and the harder you search for the answers, the more elusive they become. This only makes you dig your heels in deeper as you work even more relentlessly to find the solutions. Yup. That's exactly where I was. I felt hopeless, frustrated, confused, and angry.

One particular night as I drove home from work, once again desperately questioning how and when I would find the answers to my thyroid medication challenges, a shocking thought stopped me in my tracks: what if my symptoms of fatigue, lethargy, and brain fog had nothing to do with my medication needing to be corrected and everything to do with the situation guiding me in a different direction? In an instant, I knew this to be true. All the cells in my body began to vibrate in recognition of this truth.

Given my background as a clinical social worker and naturopathic doctor, emotional health has always been integral to my work with patients. But in the prior few years, I'd come to understand just how intertwined physical and emotional health are. I'd witnessed in myself and my patients the power of wholeheartedly addressing emotional health when chronic illness is present. When emotional health is not addressed, it becomes so much harder for lasting healing to occur. Yet when it's included, holy cow, it's a game changer. And *this* is what I'd been feeling called to focus on for some time. Yet I was scared. I didn't know what it would look like or how I would make the professional shift happen, which left me paralyzed. Until the night I drove home from the office and found myself wondering if the challenges with my body post-thyroidectomy were a result of resisting my internal nudges to head in a new direction professionally.

I returned home that evening and informed my wife that I was ready to make this professional shift. She was shocked by my sudden clarity but not surprised by the details of it, as she'd been encouraging me to make this shift for a couple of years. In fact, I suspect she was thinking, "Well, phew. It's about damn time!" Over the next few weeks, I informed my patients of my intended shift in focus and took the necessary steps to implement things. While nothing had changed with my thyroid medication, I had more energy, could think clearly, and function again more easily.

Here's what I've learned: it's human to want to deem our unwanted experiences and emotions definitively wrong. Yet this often has the unexpected result of cutting us off from other possibilities, awarenesses, or understandings. But sometimes, we still need to make things wrong for a while, which is exactly what I did on and off throughout my cancer journey (and still do sometimes). Each time I shifted from a lens of wrongness, when I could only see how wrong the given situation was, and invited in a lens of curiosity, something changed for me. This enabled me to experience cancer without demonizing it. I didn't intend to do that, but that's what happened. When I didn't demonize my cancer, this created room for me to understand my cancer cells in a new way, as confused cells. That even made it possible to appreciate and love those confused cancer cells. My sweet, cancerous thyroid taught me how possible it is to have a different experience with just about *anything* in our lives when we shift the lens we use to one that invites curiosity instead of automatic wrongness.

Chapter Two

THE ART OF BODY-DISREGARDING

The spring quarter of my junior year in college, I left school early with mononucleosis. My dad drove the five hours to pick me up, and my mom sent him with a homemade sign that read, "SWOLLEN SPLEEN." Two safety pins accompanied this sign, along with an additional note instructing me to attach it to the front of my shirt and wear it for the duration of the ride home in case we were in a car wreck. We knew a family who had recently lost their only child to a ruptured spleen post-mononucleosis. In my family, we liked to be prepared for any possible perils, so if one showed up, we'd be ready. My mom wasn't messing around.

Upon returning home, I endured daily fevers, body aches, swollen glands, and insomnia despite my utter exhaustion. I lay low for a week or two. But then, that little inner voice began to harass me. It declared, "Uh oh. You're getting lazy. You're not doing enough. You're just lying around. You're being narcissistic." My mom is a psychotherapist, so my sisters and I were familiar with the word narcissism from an early age. It equated with extreme self-centeredness in our minds and, from our perspective, was likely the worst thing we could be.

As this inner voice harangued me, my ability to lie low waned as the inner pressure to do and help and accomplish grew. It wasn't long before I took on the self-assigned project of organizing our family attic. I grew up in a 150-year-old rectory next door to the Episcopal church, where my dad was the rector. Our attic was at the top of a narrow, steep staircase. It was of notable size, with lots of nooks and crannies, which meant it had lots of space to stash stuff. It had become a receptacle for many items over the years, both big and small: old books, boxes of clothes we'd outgrown, suitcases, furniture, etc. And with the busyness of life and a house full of three growing kids, these things ended up in the attic in great disarray.

Well, amidst my mono symptoms, I attacked that attic like it was my business. I hauled my exhausted body up and down those stairs each day, moving furniture, going through boxes, purging old books and school papers. I dusted, vacuumed, and reorganized the whole damn thing. I worked on that attic for hours each day over numerous weeks. It didn't matter that my body ached, my glands throbbed, or my fever remained because I was really good at disregarding my body. I just didn't know it.

I'll bet you're familiar with body-disregarding, even if you've never before thought about it that way. Much of the time, it results in accolades from others. Isn't that wild? When a person, especially a woman, pushes herself to accomplish something despite how exhausted, ill, anxious, or depressed she is, others cheer her on. They proclaim, "Wow. Look at you go, even when you're so exhausted and juggling so many other responsibilities. You still find a way to make this happen. You're amazing!" Our culture fosters this, especially in women. It's been so insidiously woven into our experiences that it's easy for us to miss.

There's another aspect of this dynamic we easily overlook. If accolades are offered for disregarding our bodies in the name of accomplishing and helping, what does that say about the experience our bodies are having? It certainly doesn't suggest the body's experience is valued. Instead, respect and appreciation are clearly placed on the act of doing and accomplishing. If we take it even further, this suggests that the body's experience is not only of lesser value but could even be considered altogether wrong.

There I was in the throes of mono, fulfilling this cultural expectation to do and accomplish while feeling convinced that my body's illness was wrong. It was something in my way. And this is a belief I carried back into my senior year of college, where my symptoms of mono persisted. My body continued to ache. My daily, low-grade fevers remained. My glands throbbed. My energy remained nonexistent. Yet I pushed through this last year of school, continuing classes, extracurricular and social activities, and completing applications for graduate school. The accolades continued. "How do you do it? You're amazing!" I was pushing past my body's cues to keep on doing and accomplishing.

Mind you, this is not a criticism of those who offer accolades for this kind of behavior. I was one of those accolade-giving people for many years. It's simply an ingrained response in our culture, especially when it comes to women, so it's easy for us to miss the other messages we're sending when we cheer others on for accomplishing while disregarding their bodies.

THE RELENTLESS INNER WAR

The year after I graduated from college, I continued as I had in the early throes of navigating those mono symptoms. This subsequently morphed into a chronic illness that lasted another eight years and completely altered the life I'd known. My body ached continuously, and I had daily migraines and low-grade fevers. Dizziness and nausea frequently owned me. My legs felt like lead. I lost thirty pounds in one year and had started already slender. My energy was so low that I unintentionally fell asleep at the kitchen table countless times.

Yet many of the doctors I consulted disregarded my physical symptoms, having no explanation for them, and repeatedly suggested a psychiatric consult would be more helpful.

Even though I was a skilled body-disregarder myself, when faced with medical specialists who further dismissed my body's experience, it was devastating, enraging, and confusing. I knew what I was experiencing, yet these doctors insisted no identifiable illness was present. And yes, of course, depression wormed its way in. Over those last two years, I'd completely lost the Emily I knew. I went to psychiatrists who gave me antidepressants. The medication helped me feel I might survive the hell in which I found myself, but it didn't alter my physical symptoms, which made me double down on my efforts to find the answers to my mysterious illness. It was eventually diagnosed as chronic fatigue and immune dysfunction syndrome (CFIDS) in 1995, a relatively new diagnosis with few known treatments and a lifetime prognosis.

I pushed on, working toward my master's degree in social work, barking at my body to keep going and to stop with the symptoms because I didn't have time for them. There was no way I would give in to a body that was betraying me.

I was at war with my body. You may know this experience, too, whether it's your physical health or some other unwelcome experience like anxiety. You feel desperate to understand. You search for the medical fixes. Maybe you try therapy. And when that doesn't work, you expand your circle of possibilities and start exploring alternative solutions you'd once have brushed off in a second flat.

You read books that offer endless theories about what's driving your condition. Maybe you find a book that says you need to reduce your stress, so, you increase your self-care tools, taking this on like it's another project to accomplish. Or maybe another book says you need to let go of your resentments toward others, so you can heal. You promptly start making long lists of all those you resent, and one by one, you try to release those darn resentments.

Maybe it helps. A little. For a while. But then some of your symptoms return. And you feel deflated. Helpless. Hopeless. *Pissed* that your body isn't responding. And the war resumes.

LENS OF WRONGNESS

I lived this way for many of the years of my twenties. But the body isn't the only thing with which we can go to war. This inner fight can just as easily happen with many other aspects of ourselves and our experiences because our culture promotes a lens of wrongness. We silently learn to believe that any undesirable facets of who we are, what we feel, or what we experience are innately wrong and require that we go to war against them, searching outside ourselves for ways to fix or escape this assumed wrongness. Discovering this lens of wrongness damn well changed my life, and it just might change yours too.

Before you start to worry that I'm suggesting an experience like CFIDS—let alone any other illness—is a fabulous thing to go through, I'm not. It was hellish moving through that period of my life. But believing my body betrayed me changed how I moved through that journey and not in a helpful way. I can look back now and recognize how this lens of wrongness I view my illness through prevented me from noticing how my body was trying to guide me back home to myself, where possibilities, clarity, and healing are more easily born.

In my seventeen years as a practicing physician, I've worked with thousands of patients navigating illness. I've consistently shared my belief that the body communicates with us in symptoms. The tricky part is that it doesn't speak our native tongue, so we need to try and translate. Yet, in truth, for many of those earlier years as a doc, I still joined my patients in using a lens of wrongness. I viewed their symptoms as inherently wrong and looked for the fixes. I didn't yet know the power of pausing in the micro-moment to become curious about the possibility their bodies might be guiding us toward understanding and healing in ways that didn't require we make them wrong.

Does this mean searching for the fix is wrong? No, but when we automatically make ourselves and our experiences wrong, our journey toward healing is so much more uncomfortable.

DISCOVERING YOU'RE RIGHT WHEN YOU FEEL SO WRONG

Let me share with you the story of a patient I worked with after I discovered the lens of wrongness in my own life, as it will demonstrate the powerful difference this awareness can make. Trudy (name and details have been changed to protect patient confidentiality) was a fifty-five year old woman who lived in California. She was referred to me by a previous patient. She'd worked as a therapist for eighteen years but had been on leave for the past two years due to symptoms consistent with diagnoses of fibromyalgia and chronic fatigue syndrome (CFS). In our initial consultation via Zoom, she shared how understandably betrayed she felt by her body. Her fatigue was relentless, causing significant weakness, and her brain fog made regular communication with family and friends almost impossible. She'd already consulted many conventional docs and numerous fibromyalgia/CFS specialists. She was bedbound and required care from family to assist her in activities of daily living. Of course, she was angry with her body and felt betrayed!

"What was your life like before?" I asked her. She noted she was always on the go, the kind of person everyone counted on. She always found a way to show up for anyone in need, no matter what was going on for her. She mentioned her deep frustration with having to go on leave from her job, noting how hard it was to let her clients down. She mentioned her husband's affair three years earlier, explained it was brief and had been hard at the time, but they'd both recovered from it. She was grateful for all the ways her husband was currently helping her through her illness.

Our initial consultation was meant to last one hour. Instead, fifteen minutes into our call, it was necessary to end it due to her inability to remain awake. She apologized profusely.

Over the next month, our phone visits remained short. She repeatedly criticized her body and its responses, as her mind swirled with fear that her condition was here to stay. You see, when intolerable experiences show up, it's our natural human instinct to do whatever it takes to get away from the discomfort, rid ourselves of it, or find the fix. Our minds take over, future-tripping and spinning with fear. And before we know it, the tension in the body and mind quadruple, believing there is a war at hand that must be fought.

But sometimes relief is found in the micro-moment, perched just inside, waiting for you to come home. I don't mean a miraculous relief that results in spontaneous healing. I'm talking about a relief that becomes possible inside oneself *while* navigating something unwanted such as chronic illness.

I began to invite Trudy to come back home to herself for mere micro-moments. What did this coming home look like? It looked like pauses throughout our sessions whenever she noticed her brain shutting down. We started making that shutdown right instead of wrong and would pause, sometimes for five minutes, sometimes for the day. She slowly began to experience her symptoms as guidance from her body instead of another assault. Notice the shift away from the lens of wrongness? This often meant our visits were a total of five to ten minutes during that first month or two. But each time a pause was necessary, I celebrated her acknowledgment of this.

I thanked her body for being so clear with us about its needs. And we honored the heck out of it in that micro-moment.

We also began to make room for many other unwelcome experiences that showed up in our sessions, like sadness, anxiety, fear, and anger. Her own lens of wrongness taught her to make these emotions wrong and fight against them. I showed her how to turn toward these emotions for seconds and communicate with them instead of immediately making them wrong. This allowed a momentary pause for her to be present with her feelings without having to fix them or make them go away.

As we played with this, Trudy started to experience moments and then hours of relief from her symptoms. Our sessions began to last longer. Her energy slowly improved. Her ability to connect with others once again became more possible, as did her ability to spend windows of time out of bed. She continued to practice using this new lens in her life. She didn't always remember to pause the fight against the unwanted experience and turn toward it for a moment. The good news is, that kind of perfection isn't one bit necessary for this act of coming home to be impactful. We get to be our imperfect human selves and still reap the benefits of shifting from a lens of wrongness into curiosity even if we don't remember to make this shift all the time.

CURIOSITY AS AN ANTIDOTE

Over the two years that Trudy and I worked together, she continued to practice the shift from a lens of wrongness into one of curiosity in the micro-moments of her life.. This made room for her to acknowledge her anger toward her husband and his affair without needing to fix this anger or get rid of it. There was space for her to feel her incredible grief about the stark changes in her life and feel hope for her recovery at the same time. She began to recognize her lifelong habit of disregarding her own needs and feelings, often for the perceived sake of others. And her body's symptoms began to have a different meaning. Instead of simply being a betrayal, they were a call for her to come back home to herself and value her own needs as much as others.

Upon shifting from this lens of wrongness that innately created a war within her, a new relationship with herself was born. This relationship allowed her to tap into the treasure trove of guidance and clarity woven throughout her symptoms. Up to this point, she'd spent a lifetime taking care of others at a cost to herself. She'd learned to disregard her own needs and quiet nudges from her body until the those nudges became loud screams, forcing her to a complete halt. Does this mean all she needed to do was come back home to herself to be magically healed? Nah. Does it mean her ability to tune in to her inner guidance and honor the nudges from her body and soul made her journey through the intolerable experiences less wrong and less hellish? Yup. And this made her healing more possible than when she was in a war with herself.

It's so human to navigate life with a lens of wrongness. It's an approach we were born into as a culture. And because most individuals around us are using this lens, too, it's no wonder we have no idea of the inner war it cultivates in each of us. But it's this inner fight that further complicates those unwelcome experiences we're trying so hard to get out of, fix, or eradicate.

When I first discovered my own lens of wrongness, I was determined to eliminate it from my life. Who wants unwelcome experiences to be even harder than they already are? My own lens of wrongness still shows up in my life all the time. But you know what else shows up as I practice coming back home to myself in the micro-moments of my day? A growing ability to more quickly notice when I've returned to using this lens. I can feel it in my body. That wrongness lens cultivates an inner war between myself and my unwelcome experiences. Suddenly, I'm fighting against my anxiety, grief, anger, confusion, sore throat, migraine, etc. My shoulders climb up to my ears. My jaw clenches tighter. My mind spins as it desperately searches for how to get rid of what I'm feeling or experiencing. And my nervous system shifts into all-out stress mode.

There are a billion different ways a lens of wrongness can be applied to our lives. Anxiety is surely one area. Together, anxiety and I spent a lifetime cohabitating, yet I went to war against her. Illness, people-pleasing, perfectionism, fear, uncertainty, and even aging are other experiences that easily drive us to make them wrong. And to fight against them. But what if it turns out that learning to come back home to ourselves with curiosity in micro-moments literally paves the way to discovering our rightness? It's been perched inside the parts of our lives that have felt wrong for so long. I continuously find this to be true both professionally and personally.

Chapter Three

HOW TO EXPERIENCE THE POWER OF THE MICRO-MOMENT... RIGHT NOW

Let's talk more about this micro-moment business. What does it *really* mean to pause in a micro-moment? And how could something so brief be so powerful?

Let's try something together right now that will help it make more sense. I want you to make a fist with one hand. This fist represents whatever unwelcome emotion or experience you're currently navigating and wanting to fix or eliminate. Maybe it's anxiety, anger, or grief. Perhaps it's a hard decision you have to make. Maybe it's frustration with your spouse or job. With your other hand, I want you to try to pry your fist open. Notice how your fist responds. Does it easily unfold as the other hand works to pry it open? More likely, you notice your fist tighten against the prying. And how does your other hand feel as it's prying your fist? You probably notice the hand becomes frustrated and more determined to force the fist open.

OK, now shake out your hands. Make a fist again. This fist still represents whatever unwanted emotion or experience you're currently navigating and working hard to fix or eliminate. Take your other hand and instead of trying to pry the fist open, rest your fist in the palm of your other hand and allow that other hand to gently hold your fist. Notice how your fist responds to this. And how your other hand feels as it gently cups and supports your clenched fist. More than likely, you notice your fist relaxing and uncurling a bit. And the fight between the two hands softens and dissolves, unlike in the first scenario.

This example reflects what can happen when we rest in the micro-moment. This pause makes it possible to momentarily suspend the fight that naturally shows up when we use a lens of wrongness. Instead of increased tension, there's more space for clarity, guidance, and relief to slip in.

How the Micro-Moment Can Ease Inner Conflict

Let me share an example of how this looks in real life. I'd been working with Maria (name and details have been changed to protect patient confidentiality) for six months when she found herself in a state of great conflict. She'd worked in the insurance industry for over twenty years and enjoyed her work. She was eligible for a promotion that would require her to complete additional coursework and a lengthy exam. She was an intelligent woman and knew she'd do well in this coursework, but it would require months of study and time. Colleagues frequently commended her on her gifts in their industry. They knew she was eligible for this promotion and that she was a shoo-in once the necessary pre-reqs were completed. They assumed she wanted it and regularly chatted with her about how perfect she would be for this new role. But here's the catch. Once she signed up for the coursework and started her studies, she began questioning her genuine desire for the promotion. She felt confused by this. She knew she was an obvious choice for the job and understood why. Yet a small inner voice quietly asked, "Do you really want this?" This question left her guilty. Others believed in her, and they expected her to want this new position. She worried she would disappoint those who'd gone to bat for her and those who expected her to take the promotion. Refusing the promotion seemed ridiculous. She remained convinced the solution to this conflict lay somewhere outside her.

This inner conflict only grew with time. Her lens of wrongness was in full gear as she struggled to change how she felt, viewing her growing questions about this promotion as wrong. She continued to study for her coursework but grew increasingly anxious, resulting in a spinning mind that regularly searched for how to fix this struggle, often leading to frustrating insomnia.

Maria and I continued to meet during this time. I invited her to tune in to her *Micro-Moment Meter*. She noticed what it felt like in her body when she pushed on with her studies in the face of her doubt about wanting the promotion. She realized her chest felt tighter and her shoulders hiked up to her ears. It was more difficult to concentrate, which pissed her off and made her push harder to study. I asked her to tune in to any words her inner bully might be saying to her during this. Pausing in that micro-moment to think about it, she realized her inner bully repeatedly cried out, "What's wrong with you? This is ridiculous. Of *course* you want this promotion. It's what you've always wanted, and it's what others expect you to do too. The promotion makes sense. Stop questioning it and just study already. You're wasting time."

As Maria navigated this internal conflict using a lens of wrongness, it reflected the same experience of the hand working terribly hard to pry the fist open. Everything tightened and grew stressful. She was convinced she needed to force herself to study, seeing no other choice. Her ability to see other possibilities was notably limited because of her lens of wrongness and the resulting inner war between herself and her doubts.

That's the power of tuning into the micro-moment. It enabled Maria to notice what it felt like *in* her body when she disregarded her doubt and pushed forward to study anyway. The micro-moment pause invited her from up in the attic of her spinning mind and down into her body. It also offered her new awareness of her inner bully's words, which had slipped in under her radar until then.

I taught Maria how to check in with her inner *Micro-Moment Meter* as she navigated her confusion. She closed her eyes and imagined herself already in the new position at work. I invited her to notice whether her body felt more relaxed and free or tense and stressed when she thought about this. She noticed it felt more tense. I asked her to imagine turning down the promotion and notice what she felt in her body. She noticed her body felt more relaxed.

These were helpful clues for Maria, but they didn't leave her with the clarity she wanted. This was not a problem, though, because there were eons of micro-moments ahead of her in which she could check in with her *Micro-Moment Meter*, which naturally leads to more clarity with ease instead of struggle. And this is exactly what she did. She woke up each day, ready to study. But before sitting down to do so, she paused for a micro-moment or two to notice whether her body felt more relaxed or tense at the thought of studying that day. Some days, she felt relaxed at the thought of it, so she tackled the books like it was nobody's business. Other days, even wondering about studying made her feel tense and stressed. At first, she was able to notice when she felt tense, but it was too difficult to turn away from her studies, so she persisted. As she practiced this tool each morning, she noticed the days she studied when relaxed were more pleasurable than those when she studied feeling stressed and tense. This realization led her to change up her response to her *Micro-Moment Meter* findings.

Maria continued to take micro-moments each morning to tune in to her inner meter, but on the days the thought of studying made her feel tense and stressed, she purposely chose *not* to study. And oh, boy, was this uncomfortable for her to do at first, but her energy began to increase. Her mood felt lighter on those days. A peculiar sense of hope slipped in, but about what she wasn't even sure. She practiced this way for about three weeks, honoring the clues her body offered each morning. Around that twenty-first day, she woke up, checked in with herself and her body, and knew with 100 percent clarity that she did not want to take that promotion. She experienced an absolute knowing about this in every cell of her body and promptly boxed up her course-work and threw it in the trash. She informed her bosses and colleagues of her decision, which surprised many of them, but their quick acceptance of her decision stunned her, given her anticipatory anxiety about this a few weeks earlier.

Do you know why it was possible for Maria to move into this absolute knowing? Because those micro-moments in which she checked in with herself and her inner meter each morning were equivalent to shifting from trying to pry her fist open to gently supporting her fist in exactly the state it was in. Those instances of coming home paused the inner war against her unwanted feelings. This pause was sometimes only seconds long, but that's all it takes to shift away from a lens of wrongness and into a space of curiosity. And curiosity, well, that's a damn game changer, folks. Her daily moments of genuine curiosity about her inner experience allowed her to honor her nudges instead of quickly disregarding them or trying to make them go away. It allowed her to turn *toward* those undesirable feelings with curiosity instead of away from them with a fight. And turning toward our unwanted emotions or experiences in the micro-moment creates space for new guidance, nudges, and clarity to slip in with ease.

MICRO-MOMENT METER

- This is particularly helpful to use when you are faced with a decision or are in confusion about something. The decision can be as big as whether to take a new job or as small as whether to watch TV or go to bed, or whether to wear your red or blue shirt. As you practice checking in with your *Micro-Moment Meter*, your ability to tune in to your nudges and inner guidance is strengthened. It need only be employed in micro-moments over time, enabling you to move into more clarity. A bonus is that feelings are not disregarded to come to the answer more quickly.

- Bring to mind one of the choices you are facing. For simplicity, if you are struggling to decide whether to wear your red or blue shirt, take a micro-moment to pause and imagine yourself wearing the red shirt.

- Drop your focus from up in the attic of your mind and down into your body. Notice whether wearing this red shirt makes you feel more relaxed and free or tense and stressed inside your body.

- Next, try on the blue shirt in your mind. Drop your focus down into your body and notice whether this shirt leads you to feel more relaxed or stressed.

- You may realize you feel more relaxed when you imagine wearing the blue shirt, but because others expect you to wear the red shirt, it feels impossible to go with the choice that makes you feel relaxed. That's totally OK. Celebrate the fact that you can notice which one feeds your soul more, but also honor that choosing the shirt that makes you feel lighter is too scary, uncomfortable, or difficult in that moment.

- As you continue to play with this tool in different micro-moments of your days, you will find your ability to turn toward the more relaxed choice becomes more possible without forcing it to happen. This is exactly why it can be helpful to start out using this tool with the smaller decisions in your life. It builds your ability to recognize the guidance being offered by your inner compass and grows the trust you have in yourself. Then, when the bigger choices show up, navigating them begins to happen with more ease.

USING THE MICRO-MOMENT WHEN YOU'RE TRIGGERED

Maria's way of pausing in the micro-moment isn't the *only* way to do so! Gosh, that's what's so powerful about it. There are many ways to harness the micro-moment in our lives. And various ways are helpful to different people.

The *Micro-Moment Reset* is another approach I initially created for myself while learning how to navigate my anxiety. In chapter nine, I'll go into more detail about my lifelong experience with anxiety and how my relationship with it transformed, but I'll mention here that this *Micro-Moment Reset* played an important role in that transformation.

I invite you to download the free audio of this *Micro-Moment* Reset at https://dremilycolwell.com/free-gift/ or scan the QR code in the back of this book. Many find it particularly helpful to have guidance through the steps in an audio format to more easily begin to use it on their own. This practice can be particularly helpful when you are feeling gripped about something, stuck, stressed, or anxious. Or if you're feeling angry, sad, or even confused. The mind often spins as it searches for the solutions that will get you out of the unwanted situation and away from the unwelcome feelings that come with it. You might even notice that the harder you try to find the solutions, the worse you feel. It's often in these moments when you're simply trying to push through it all that your body begins to have symptoms too. Your jaw becomes clenched, your shoulders hike up to your ears, your neck tightens. Maybe a stomachache starts or a headache oozes in. And these symptoms feel *so wrong*! And you push harder and try to disregard them.

What if it turns out these symptoms and uncomfortable emotions are simply messengers trying to get our attention? And no, it doesn't have to mean they're trying to tell us we're going in the wrong direction. Often, it's an invitation for us to pause in this micro-moment and come back home to ourselves. Creating these micro-moment pauses makes it so much more possible for us to move into relief, feel more ease, and find more clarity without working so hard to make this happen. And the best part is that relief stops being dependent upon your external circumstances changing.

For those of you for whom this *Micro-Moment Reset* is a good fit, you'll likely come out of this exercise feeling a weight has been lifted from your shoulders. It may be easier to take a deep breath. You will likely notice a decrease in how gripped you feel about the particular circumstances you're in. And the emotions that felt like they owned you will feel far more manageable. This *Micro-Moment Reset* can last for as little as a few seconds or for minutes or longer. It all depends upon what feels good to you in this specific moment and with this particular emotion.

MICRO-MOMENT RESET

(Available for download in audio format here: https://dremilycolwell. com/free-gift/ or by scanning the QR code in the back of this book)

- Find a seated or lying position that feels comfortable to you. This can be done lying on your bed, sitting in a chair, parked in your car, or even seated on the toilet in a public restroom!

- I want you to tune in to what you're feeling emotionally. Sometimes it's helpful to briefly bring to mind the circumstances that have you feeling gripped. This can help you more easily notice the emotion showing up for you in this moment. You don't even have to name the feeling or know exactly why you're feeling it.

- Simply notice the loudest emotion you are experiencing. Once you find it, I want you to gently lift up the story about why you are feeling this way or what caused it. I want you to place the story off to the side for the next few minutes.

- Now close your eyes and begin to softly scan your body and tune in to where in your body this emotion is espe- cially strong. Is it in the pit of your stomach? Your chest? Your throat? Your shoulders? Is it in your head? In your wrists or ankles? Maybe you feel it everywhere. There is no wrong answer here.

- Once you notice where it's especially strong in your body, begin to imagine what this feeling looks like. Does it have a shape? You may see circles or cells. Or perhaps you see another image. Does it have a color? Maybe it has a tex- ture or a smell. Is it a specific size? If there's more than one image that you are seeing, are the images close together or far apart? Is the image vibrating or moving, or is it com- pletely still? If it's moving, does the movement seem to be rhythmic or chaotic? There's no wrong answer here either. Each person experiences this in their own way.

- As you hold this image in your mind, envision the image in the middle of a field or a clearing.

- Check in with yourself to see if it feels more comfortable to go plop down right next to this image in the middle of the field. Or if you would prefer to sit at the edge of the clearing, where you can still see the image but you don't have to be so close to it. There is no pressure for you to be closer to the image if that does not feel comfortable. Honor what feels the best to you at this moment.

- In your mind, begin to imagine talking to this image you're seeing. See how it feels to say to this image, "I'm just going to sit here with you while you're feeling whatever you're feeling. And whatever you're feeling right now in this moment is *totally* OK. And I'm just going to sit here with you while you're feeling it."

- For some, this feels comfortable to say. If you are someone for whom this feels uncomfortable, try saying this instead, "This feels really uncomfortable for me to be here right now so I'm gonna sit on the edge of the field where I can see you, but I don't have to be so close. And I want you to know that I'm going to sit over here and be present from the edge while you're feeling whatever you're feeling."

- And then do just that. Quietly sit in the presence of this image and periodically remind it that you are simply sitting with it while it feels whatever it's feeling and that any feeling it has is totally OK in this moment.

- There's no need to try to change the feeling or make it go away. Simply acknowledging its presence and how it feels in this micro-moment is what makes this exercise helpful.

- Some of you may notice the image begins to change from its original form, while others won't. There's no wrong way to experience this.

- You may notice that the image begins to move or vibrate in a different way. The shape or colors you're seeing may shift a bit.

- Continue to remind the image that you are present with it and whatever it's feeling *now* is totally OK in this moment.

- You may feel called to check in with the image and ask it if it would like you to stay present with it for a few more minutes. Sometimes you'll sense this is helpful. Other times it won't be necessary.

- You are welcome to stay in the field with this image for as long as it feels comfortable to you. Some notice the image begins to disappear or their attention begins to lose its focus. All of these responses are great. Again, there's no wrong response here.

- When you feel ready, open your eyes and go on with your day!

WHAT PART OF YOU IS VISITING?

Another way to experience the power of the micro-moment that can be particularly helpful to explore is the *Who's Knocking?* technique. But before I go into detail about this, let me give you some background.

We each have an outer family. For some, we were born into this family. For others, we were adopted or fostered into it, or we formed this family through choice. Well, I've come to understand that we have an inner family that resides inside us too. This inner family is made up of many different parts of us that formed through a multitude of experiences in our lives and developed beliefs that at one point or another helped us cope or survive. But here's something to remember about some of these inner parts: they show up with emotions we *don't* want to have around. How do we know when they're present? When an uninvited emotion shows up and becomes louder and louder in our lives. That's an inner part yelling for our attention. For example, in Maria's story above, the longer she experienced conflict about her potential promotion, the louder her feelings of wrongness became. Her doubt about taking that new position felt increasingly wrong, so all she wanted to do was get rid of the doubt. But the harder she worked to rid herself of it, the louder the conflict and doubt. That was an inner part of her attempting to get her attention with the notable doubt and fear the part was experiencing.

When these *unwanted* parts of us show up like this, our natural human instinct is to fight against them. But here's the tricky part. The more we fight against them, the more this engages our fight-or-flight stress response. And the more these parts attempt to get our attention. But it turns out these parts of us have *no* interest in being fixed. They simply want to be seen by us. They instinctively know that this is where the possibility of relief is born. Yet we often spend a lifetime feeling at war with these unwanted parts, thus keeping them at a distance and chronically activating the stress response in the body. It is through the process of learning how to acknowledge these parts and whatever they're feeling in the micro-moment that allows the grip they have on us to begin to soften and dissolve. This is so counterintuitive.

The cool thing about discovering you have a whole tribe of inner family members or parts is that this opens the door to a shift from being at war with some of them to building a relationship with them. And these relationships turn out to be monumentally life-changing as they make room for these inner parts to ultimately update their beliefs. They can then integrate into who you are, bringing with them many gifts to which you previously had little access.

So how do you access these parts? Good question. The truth is there are many ways. The *Who's Knocking?* technique is a light, simple way to do this. And just as I mentioned about the *Micro-Moment Meter* and the *Micro-Moment Reset*, this technique also works extremely well for some and is not a fit for others, so play with the following and notice what feels true for you.

WHO'S KNOCKING?

- Imagine you are safely at home by yourself when you hear a knock at your door. When you open that door, standing there will be a part of you that is feeling whatever unwanted emotion is particularly loud in you. If it's helpful, you can imagine yourself approaching the door not as the person feeling those unwanted feelings but as your connected or higher self.

- When you open the door, notice what you find on the other side. For some, a person shows up. For others, the part shows up as a shape, image, cartoon character, or color. And others simply sense the presence of the visiting part of them.

- If the part shows up for you with a physical presence, notice how the part looks, if it has a gender, if it's standing close to the door, or has it knocked and then backed way up? Does this part have an expression on its face? What kind of body language does this part have?

- If the part shows up as a color or image, notice any details that stand out to you.

- Once you've noticed the above, greet this part and acknowledge how it seems to be feeling. Don't try to fix the feeling. Simply be present with this part while it's feeling.

- Check in to see if there's anything that would enable this part to feel more at ease as you connect with it. Does this part want to sit on the stoop with you or come inside for hot cocoa? Does it want to go on a walk or to the park with you? Does this part seem guarded and unready to come any closer? *Any* of these responses from this part are perfect.

- If the part seems willing to connect, try asking it if there's anything it wants you to know or wants to share with you. Sometimes you will be surprised by what these parts have to share.

- It's often helpful to say some version of the following to the part: "I want you to know that I didn't realize you've been in here all this time. And now that I do, I want to learn how to show up for you. There's a good chance I'm gonna mess up sometimes as I'm learning how to do this, but I want you to know that my intention remains to learn how to show up for you instead of fighting to make you go away." Notice how this part responds when you say this. For my fellow perfectionists or recovering perfectionists out there, it can be a surprising relief to discover how accepting these parts are to our acknowledgment that we may sometimes mess up as we learn how to connect with them! This reflects their acceptance of our imperfectness as well as their number one need: to be seen rather than fixed by us.

- If the part is reticent or downright opposed to connecting, it can be helpful to check in to see if this part would be open to you leaving it with an animal. I know this may sound unexpected and strange, but some of these parts find it incredibly reassuring, and it helps them feel less alone but also makes it acceptable for them to feel reticent about connecting with you. The good news? You're not limited by your choice of animals. Sometimes it's a cat or dog. And sometimes it's a mama baboon as it was for one of my inner family members I came to know. See what shows up!

- If the part has no interest in an animal and no interest in connecting, see if you can make room for this the way you might with a resistant teenager because we all know that pushing a defensive teenager to be less defensive *never* works!

- Feel your way through your time with this part in the same way you would in any new relationship. Notice when to move forward and connect more and when to back up.

- As long as it feels comforting to connect with the part, feel free to spend those micro-moments together. If it immediately feels uncomfortable for you or becomes uncomfortable, close that door. It even works to tell the part that it feels too scary to connect at that moment but that you intend to come back when it feels more possible. The amount of time you spend connecting with an inner part is not what matters the most. It's that you took a step to turn toward this part instead of away from it that has the most powerful impact over time.

- When you feel it's time to close the door, feel free to tell the part you will be back again. Then close that door, understanding that when those unwanted feelings show up in you again, it's simply this part coming for a visit and wanting your acknowledgment.

Can you see how we can experience the power of the micro-moment? It invites us to come home to ourselves, sometimes for a mere second or two. But even seconds allow new neural pathways to start forming, ultimately offering the mind new choices and reactions when faced with unwelcome experiences and emotions. The mind begins to notice that making these unwanted moments wrong, and fighting against them, only makes the experience harder and prolonged. But turning toward these instances with curiosity, even for a moment, births the possibility of relief that was once nowhere in sight. This process is known as neuroplasticity, which refers to our brain's incredible ability to change and rewire itself. Neural pathways are like a network of roads in our brain where our thoughts and feelings travel. And neuroplasticity allows the brain to renovate, adapt and reshape these pathways so we can ultimately navigate emotions and challenging experiences with more ease.

Let me give you an example that reflects how neuroplasticity works to create, strengthen, or weaken these pathways to help make life easier for us. Imagine walking in the woods along a familiar, well-trodden path—one you traverse daily without much thought. Despite hearing about a beautiful grove hidden within the woods, you persist in taking the familiar route because there's no trail to the hidden spot. But one day, you decide to break the routine and shake things up. You start forging your way through the dense undergrowth, contending with branches, fallen trees, and even poison ivy. You wander a bit further each time, until one day, you discover the beautiful cluster of trees. Each time you return to this peaceful spot, your footsteps leave ever-deepening marks on the forest floor. As you repeatedly come back to this path that was once challenging and unknown, it gradually transforms into a clear, well-worn trail, offering a new way through the woods.

So, think of neuroplasticity as this cool brain superpower. It's all about how our brain deals with the emotions and situations we face in life. Using a lens of wrongness drives us to react in ways that are familiar and automatic, just like taking the well-worn path in the woods. It doesn't matter if those automatic responses make the experience harder, because our brain is convinced there's no other possible response to have.

But here's the exciting part: if we shake things up and approach those times with curiosity, even just a bit, it's like carving out a new trail in the woods. This fosters new neural pathways in the brain, enabling different responses to become increasingly possible in those tricky moments. With practice, the stuff bothering us starts losing its grip because our mind learns there are other ways to react that bring more ease.

And get this! With the help of micro-moment pauses, these new neural pathways that we cultivate don't just help us handle tough moments; they also make it easier to listen to our inner compass and find the path back home to ourselves. Yep, it turns out our brains can change! And the tools in this chapter offer a first step in making it possible for these changes to come to life.

Chapter Four

IS YOUR SECRET PREVENTING YOU FROM BEING YOUR AUTHENTIC SELF?

I grew up with a secret. The only people who knew this secret were my parents and the police. This secret guided the way I presented myself to the world. Over time, it convinced me there was a certain right way to be in the world. And it was determined by others, not me.

My secret was born when I was five years old. My dad was the Episcopal priest in our town, and I was the eldest of three daughters. We lived in the rectory next door to the church. My parents periodically held parties for visiting bishops and church parishioners, and one of those parties took place on a particular fall evening.

The church janitor, Eddie, stopped by the rectory to ask if my parents needed anything for the party. My mom realized she'd run out of ice and asked if he could bring more ice from the church freezer. I joined Eddie on this errand, feeling like a big kid, and we headed to the church kitchen together. As we approached the room outside the kitchen, he sat next to me on top of a nearby table and told me he had something special to share, asking if I was going to tell my parents. I remember curiously wondering what the right answer was. I wanted to give him the one he wanted to hear. I wanted to please him because, well, I wanted to please everyone back then. I just wasn't positive which answer would do that. I took a guess and said I wouldn't tell. My younger self went on to wonder if things might have turned out differently had I given the other answer.

As Eddie sexually abused me in the kitchen of the church that late afternoon, I remember hearing the neighborhood boys riding by on their bikes, calling to each other. A lonely feeling gathered in the pit of my stomach as I realized they had no idea I was just inside the window they were biking past. I remember feeling left out and alone. My head swirled with too many thoughts and no thoughts all at once. I felt incredible confusion. I floated up to the ceiling, watched my abuse from afar, and thought a lot about the boys biking outside.

After what felt like hours, but was likely fifteen to twenty minutes, I heard my mother calling to me as she rushed through the dark hallways of the church building. She'd been at home, frantically managing a big church party, when she instantly turned white as a ghost and cried out, "Emily!" She knew something was wrong.

When Eddie heard my mother approaching, he hurriedly yanked our pants back on and turned toward the freezer to gather the requested ice. When my mom reached the church kitchen doorway, I cried out, "Mommy, Eddie's been bad!" I assumed she wanted to know more, but she flatly replied, "Thank you for the ice, Eddie. Emily, let's go." Her response confused my little five-year-old mind. At the time, I didn't understand that a butcher knife was sitting next to me on the counter, and my mom had seen it.

She quickly walked me out of the church building and

onto a short set of steps outside one of the exits, where she sat me down and asked me to tell her what happened. I remember feeling worried that these steps were too close to the church kitchen and Eddie, but a large party was happening a mere one hundred yards away in our house.

After I explained what Eddie had done, she took me home and told my dad, who immediately charged over to the church, filled with rage, and fired him. They then bathed me, put me in a lime-green nightgown with a pale-pink rose on the left pocket, and sat me in the lap of the bishop's wife in the dining room while the party finished. All my memories of sitting on this woman's lap are from a vantage point on the ceiling, looking down at us. I didn't know what dissociating from the body was back then. But I've come to have such a tender appreciation for this skill that many of us innately harness when trauma becomes too much to handle. The tricky part arises when this dissociation tool that was once a pivotal way to survive becomes a routine way that you move through life, exiting the body and evaluating interactions and events from outside yourself rather than from inside. This was certainly my experience for *many* years, and I'll discuss how this showed up in my life in later chapters.

This was fifty years ago. Talking openly about sexual abuse was certainly not a part of the culture back then. Let's face it: it's only since the Me Too movement that this is finally changing in more significant and empowering ways. But back then, times were different. I was the Episcopal priest's kid. My parents were concerned that others would treat me differently if they knew this happened to me. As a result, they told members of the church the sexual abuse happened to an unnamed six-year-old child in the church. They told me I could talk with them about my experience anytime I wanted, but they asked me not to share it with others.

A few weeks later, I shared it with my five-year-old best friend, who promptly and smartly told his mom. His mom called my mom to let her know I must have overheard my parents talking about the six-year-old kid in the church to whom this happened. My mom agreed with her. And then reiterated to me that I could talk with them about my experience anytime but that it was better for me not to share it with others. So, I didn't. It wasn't until I was seventeen that I finally shared it with a therapist and, eventually, my younger sisters.

Unbeknownst to me, Eddie's firing triggered rage in him that led to him stalking my dad and family for another year after the abuse. We later learned he had sexually abused numerous other girls in the church over the years, but previous priests had never addressed it. While my parents chose not to press charges because this would have required that I sit in court and face Eddie again (this is no longer the case for child abuse cases, but it was back then), being held accountable when my father fired him was something that incensed Eddie. His wife called our house endless times, screaming, "Get out of the house! He's on his way over with a shotgun!" He took his family's dining room furniture into his backyard and chopped it up with an ax while declaring he was "chopping up Father Home Wrecker." He called the church and house phones, hissing rageful threats, and my parents never knew when these calls might come. The police remained closely involved throughout this time.

While I wasn't aware of this stalking until a few years later, the fear in the house was palpable. My two younger sisters and I went on to have a relentless fear that robbers might climb up the sides of our house and break into our bedroom windows. Even in the thick summer heat with no AC in the suburbs of New York City, I *always* slept under a thin sheet at the very least. Somehow this made me feel slightly safer than having nothing covering me. Even into my forties, a pervasive feeling hovered just under the surface, convincing me that a man was always about to jump out of bushes or from behind a corner and rape me in the night. As kids, we sometimes walked with a babysitter down Broadway, a main street that ran through our town. On these walks, I frequently saw these small bits of torn burlap lying on the sidewalk or the edge of the street. And I always assumed it was left over from clothing torn off women raped on Broadway late at night. Not that I'd heard that women were being raped on Broadway. I just assumed these torn pieces of burlap were proof of this. It wasn't till I was well into adulthood that I learned these pieces were from the inside of tires. You can see how pervasive my fear was.

And I was a sensitive kid. But because I didn't understand the fear, my sweet five-year-old mind created stories to explain it. One such story was related to the phone. Before the sexual abuse, I'd sometimes begun to answer the house phone, feeling like a big kid. After the sexual abuse, I was no longer allowed to answer the phone and didn't do so again until I was eight years old. Since I didn't understand why I was no longer allowed, some part of me assumed I'd wrongfully handled my earlier attempts at answering the phone. I went on to develop a phone phobia that lasted for many years. I was terrified to call almost *anyone*. Most often, I begged my younger sister to make the calls for me. But when she wouldn't or couldn't, I mapped out every word I wanted to say and wrote it all down in great detail so I could read it when I placed the call. Every muscle in my body shook from the moment I prepared to dial the number until about ten minutes after the call ended. Yet I had no understanding of why I'd developed this phobia until many years later.

My little mind created similar stories about my abuse too. While I remember telling myself that I couldn't tell others about my abuse because I didn't want them to treat me differently, my five-year-old self came to a deeper conclusion as my lens of wrongness settled in: I'd been bad beyond redemption and was now innately wrong, and my parents wanted to protect me from having others discover this.

WHEN SECRETS ALTER OUR BELIEFS

An odd thing happens with secrets, even when they're well-intentioned. They have a way of growing stories inside our minds. What can start as having simple, clear meaning can go on to hold a notably distorted perspective. I bet many of you know exactly what I'm talking about. There are so many experiences that can lead to secrecy. Sure, sexual abuse is one of them. Or living with family members in the throes of addiction, unmanaged mental illness, physical violence, or other dysfunction.

But let's be honest here. It's not always something traumatic, but a small moment, experience, or feeling that can lead to secrecy. Like telling a lie that remains with you for years to come. Maybe you developed a full-blown attraction for someone who isn't your partner. Or you didn't finish school, and it's something you try to hide from others. Perhaps you're deep in debt and afraid to have others know. Or maybe you secretly chug wine during the day but hide it from your family and friends. The list could go on.

For those who've experienced secrecy, you know its simplicity changes over time. And shame quietly weaves its way into your story. Some cut off from their secrets altogether and go on as if they never existed, but the flames of shame continue to be buried deep within you. For others, the secret comes to define you as you identify as the abused, mistreated, not good enough, or broken person. Either way, unmetabolized, leftover feelings likely leak out into other areas of your life, often impacting your relationships and how you feel in the world.

My secret made me believe that showing people my truth was a bad idea. But I had no idea I believed this. I simply experienced this belief in my body. I went to church every week and walked up the aisle for communion with my hands and legs trembling uncontrollably every ... single ... time. Yet only my sisters and my mom knew this because I was *really* good at looking like I had it all together.

I walked up that aisle worrying that others in the church pews might think my hair wasn't perfect, my outfit wasn't hip enough, my facial expression wasn't the right one, or I wasn't clasping my hands in just the right way. These same worries were present for me in the other parts of my life too. And I assumed that I trembled because I was anxious about having others' eyes on me.

What I didn't understand back then is that my secret had me convinced that the true me couldn't be shared. Instead, I believed it was necessary to create an alternate version of me that others would accept. My secret cultivated a lens of wrongness in me that I used to view myself and all that was seemingly wrong with me and needed to be hidden or fixed.

Do you know what this does to a person over time? It makes it easy to disregard your needs, wants, feelings, and questions because it's about meeting others' expectations instead of exploring your own because you're convinced yours are wrong. It becomes exhausting, constricting, and anxiety-provoking. And it places your entire focus outside of yourself. It's like living in a body, but you're not really home. And it turns out it's not particularly fun to be a human who isn't home!

My relationship with my secret, which was birthed at five-years of age, has evolved over the years. In fact, it's not even a secret anymore. In the beginning, it was *so scary* to share it with others. I was left with a panicky fear that the person listening would at the very least go on to think less of me, might pity or reject me, but would most likely feel disgusted by me. But it wasn't the sharing of my secret that changed my relationship with it. It was something else entirely.

The tiny micro-moments in which I began to invite my focus back home inside me changed the game entirely. And many of these moments lasted a mere two to three seconds in the beginning. These moments allowed me to start noticing how I truly felt about things rather than what others thought.

They created momentary space for me to tune in to whether something made me feel relaxed or tense in a given instance. It enabled me to question things in a way I'd never before done.

What did these micro-moments look like for me? Well, it depended on the day. Some days these moments created space for me to use my *Micro-Moment Meter* to tune into whether something made me feel relaxed or tense in a given instance, which offered me guidance and clarity. Other days, I paused for those few micro-moments to notice what it felt like *in my body* when that deep sense of innate wrongness overtook me. I noticed the hot wave of shame that shot through my body, the heaviness on my shoulders, the tightness in my chest, my inability to breathe deeply, and my desperate need to get rid of the feelings.

In the beginning, I could only tolerate these feelings for seconds before they became too intolerable, and I needed to shut them down, distract myself, and try to make them disappear. But those seconds were powerful. They were building my tolerance and nurturing a new neural pathway that would ultimately enable me to shift from seeing these emotions as my enemy to experiencing them as parts of me that became my teachers and guides. These micro-moments were slowly but surely shifting me from a lens of wrongness to one of curiosity, which *always* feels better. This curiosity opened me to discover that my sense of innate wrongness was simply reflecting a part of me that needed to be seen and acknowledged, not fought against. Some days, I turned toward this part of me, who believed she was shamefully wrong, and sat with her while she was feeling this. I told her I didn't want her to be alone with this heavy feeling anymore and that I wanted to show up for her during it. As I practiced this, she repeatedly sighed with relief in these moments, felt seen, and began to feel less wrong in my presence.

The *real* me began to surface in a bold and grounded new

way as I practiced these micro-moments of returning home to myself over time. Others' expectations of me gradually stopped holding the same weight as I started navigating my life from the inside out rather than from the outside in. *This* is what softened the secret within me. There was a bigger world inside me that had new depth and weight and made me feel at *home*. There was room for my wants, needs, desires, perspectives, opinions, feelings, and questions to live in me too. And this meant that my secret was no longer the loudest thing I could hear.

This is the beauty of the micro-moment. Astonishing change becomes possible through tiny steps, sometimes for mere seconds at first. These micro-moments add up over time, and they *never* have to be done perfectly or all at once to have an impact. If you're a perfectionist, this is a dream come true! Studies have shown that coming back home to ourselves and our uncomfortable feelings for a mere one to two seconds at a time begins to create new neural pathways in the brain. As these new neural pathways grow, this paves the way for new responses to old experiences. This is exactly what happened with my secret. The more I practiced returning home to myself for seconds at a time, the more I began steering my life following internal guidance rather than external influences. And *this* changed my relationship with my secret.

Now, my experience of sexual abuse no longer defines me. Instead, I'm left with incredible compassion for my young self and the journey she moved through. And I feel a surprising appreciation for the unexpected gifts that have come to me through this experience. I can see all the rightness that came out of incredible wrongness.

I've discovered that what was once a deep, dark secret for me is now something that I comfortably share with patients and others who've also experienced sexual assault in one form or another. My journey has shown me the transformational power of learning to come back home to ourselves one micro-moment at a time. And enabling that hope to be born in another person for whom it has always felt hopeless, well, how could I not wish for them to have the chance to experience this too?

Here's the deal. Coming back home to yourself makes it possible to start navigating life from the inside out so that others' expectations no longer rule your life. It makes it possible for your secrets to stop being the loudest thing driving you to create a more acceptable public version of yourself. And it makes room for you to not only feel in touch with your authentic self, but for it to comfortably shine out into the world. I was convinced that returning home to myself would only make my sense of innate wrongness so much worse. Instead, the opposite happened. The more I practiced coming back home to myself in the micro-moments, the more I tapped into my inner authentic rightness. And I'm not talking about a rigid rightness, but an aligned, embodied rightness that was felt from the inside out instead of being determined from the outside in.

If this sounds intriguing, YAHOOOO! So many of us know what it's like to haul around secrets. And these secrets can make it *so hard* to feel free to have our inside and outside versions of ourselves match. And so many of us know what it's like to view our most unwanted beliefs and feelings about ourselves as the enemy and to wage war against them. But it's possible to transform how we feel about these seemingly unwelcome parts of ourselves by harnessing the power of the micro-moment to come back home.

The good news is that you don't have to hurry up and drag those secrets out into the light of day to feel better. That becomes a natural side effect of coming back home to yourself in the micro-moment. The more this is practiced, the more your secret loses its grip on your life, the more you begin to discover all the authentic rightness that's been tucked inside your seeming wrongness, and the more at home you feel in your own body and life.

Chapter Five

DO YOU SILENTLY WORRY THAT WHO YOU ARE IS NOT OK?

I hated that I trembled. I didn't understand it, but I always knew I could count on the shaking to accompany me up and down the aisle at church each week. And because of my dad's job, I walked up that aisle for communion thousands of times! As I mentioned earlier, this wasn't a shake that others could see. No one knew I shook except my family. I'd quietly show my sisters my trembling hands and legs when we returned to our church pew each week. I hid it well and had lots of tricks to appear calm, all while my legs struggled to hold up my body.

But just like that, my shaking vanished overnight when I was thirty-eight. The evening before, I'd shared with my cousins that I was dating a woman (who went on to become my wife). They'd only known me to date men. I had, too, until three years earlier.

When I fell in love with a woman for the first time at the age of thirty-five, the life I'd come to count on abruptly felt so confusing. Seemingly out of the blue, I questioned things I'd always assumed to be true. I wasn't someone who'd knowingly had crushes on girls my whole life. Quite the opposite. I'd dated an awesome guy through four years of college and for a while afterward. We spent years planning our eventual marriage and kids. I didn't kind of love this man. I was indeed in love with him. But a relentless feeling also hovered in me, convincing me our relationship needed to be fixed in different ways. This often meant he ended up in the "doghouse," as he called it, as I repeatedly gave him one thing or another he needed to work on or get more right in our relationship. Looking back now, my heart hurts seeing how hard we both worked to "fix" things when they were never actually broken. So many parts of this relationship worked, but I believed I needed to get him to be the man I wanted him to be instead of the wonderful man he already was. And as you can imagine, that never bodes well for a happy future together.

Once we broke up, I dated a few different men. I also went on what seemed like 240,000 blind dates. So many friends and acquaintances set me up with a guy they knew or even someone their friend knew. None of these dates went anywhere. But I *will* tell you that I developed a vast array of horrifying blind-date stories that had my friends and me in fits of breathless laughter and left them begging me to write a book about all these hysterically awful dates, which hasn't yet happened, but who knows?

Throughout my life of dating men, a common thought I had was, "This could work. I could make this relationship work," all said in a flat tone inside my head. That phrase was quietly reflecting my belief that it was my job to find a way to meet external expectations because I assumed those expectations were also mine. I didn't realize then that I didn't know my inner expectations or desires. I simply knew I wanted a relationship that would look like so many of the ones I saw around me, and I assumed they also felt a certain way, and I was committed to making that happen.

You can imagine how shocked I was when I found myself attracted to a *woman*! This went against anything I'd ever imagined for myself. At first, I noticed my stomach flip over whenever this woman walked into the room or looked at me. I thought to myself, "Whoa, *that's* odd." And then I went on with my day. But it kept happening. In the same way it always happened to me when I was attracted to guys. But this time, it was a woman.

Given my early-honed skill of secret-keeping, this was a sensible time to keep this strange new reaction to myself. I felt paralyzed to share my unexpected and new experience with anyone. I could hardly make sense of what was happening, and it somehow felt wrong. I'd always stayed in touch with friends and family, yet I found myself avoiding their phone calls. I couldn't tell them about the latest turn in my life, which was an isolating, anxious, and confusing time.

I was uncertain about my identity in a way I'd never experienced. At one point, I even googled, "Am I a lesbian?" Needless to say, Google was terribly unhelpful in answering this for me. It turns out this is an answer found on the inside, not the outside. I felt fear. I felt shame. I also felt joy and a startling sense that I might be discovering a previously unseen part of myself. As my feelings for this woman grew, so did my confusion, mainly because I was once again keeping a sexually-related experience a secret from others, which automatically triggered intense shame for me. Meanwhile, as my coinciding shame and joy percolated, my crush grew and was quickly mutual.

Many hours were spent trying to make sense of what was happening to me. I moved back and forth between relishing the new, unexpected comfort and peace I'd never before experienced and the shame I would one day come to understand was partially driven by my own internalized homophobia. In my aloneness with this new experience, I sometimes chatted with God about it. In one particular conversation, it struck me, "Huh. Why would God create me with the ability to have these feelings if they were wrong? This can't be a mistake." That realization was a soothing balm in the middle of my confusion and shame.

I've always been an excellent rule follower. And dating a woman felt like I was breaking the rules. Whose rules? It would be easy to assume I was worried about religious rules, but that wasn't a loud concern. It was everyone else's rules I was concerned about. Were all these rules and expectations verbalized? No, but they didn't have to be. The unstated messages often have the most subtle but profound impact. Did I grow up seeing gay and lesbian folks? Nope. Did I know *any* gay classmates in school? Well, it turns out I *did*, but I've only come to learn that in recent years. Did I see anyone on TV who represented anything beyond the heterosexual norm? Nope. Did I hear positive stories about gay people? Nope. One story I repeatedly heard was that lesbians were sexually aggressive. And that it was sad how difficult it is for lesbians to maintain long-term relationships. Another story was that people are either born gay or become gay due to being so damaged by past trauma. As you can see, the world I grew up in had only two glaringly acceptable boxes to fit into: straight and single or straight and married. A lack of representation establishes unspoken rules and expectations about what's acceptable and what's not, and how we should or should not live our lives. And given that I'd been navigating my life from the outside in, trying like hell to figure out how I was *supposed to* live for a very long time, I'm not surprised it felt like I was breaking the rules when I fell in love with a woman for the first time.

WHOSE EXPECTATIONS ARE YOU FOLLOWING?

Have you ever felt that way? That you're expected to live your life in a certain way? Or maybe you don't even realize that outside expectations guide how you're living. Sometimes it's the only way you've ever known.

When I look back at all those times I walked up that aisle for communion and trembled as I passed parishioners in the church, I assumed my shaking was a bad thing. I was convinced I was too sensitive, and that something was wrong with me because no one else shook going up that aisle. What I didn't understand is that my trembling was a messenger clueing me into the presence of that younger part of me who learned to believe her true self was somehow wrong. The trembling reflected that this part of me was still alive inside me, believing she had to measure how she was doing according to outside expectations, whether real or imagined. It was a sign that this part of me was afraid she wouldn't get it all right and everyone would discover just how wrong she was. What I didn't understand back then was how desperately that part of me needed *me* to acknowledge her for how she was feeling so she could heal. Instead, I repeatedly believed those feelings were wrong and tried to *shut them down.*

This is what so many of us do when the messy parts of us show up. Sometimes a part shows up with anxiety or depression. Maybe it's a part of you that feels a desperate need to control things. Perhaps it's a part of you that feels worthless compared to others. Or maybe it's a part that believes it's of the utmost importance to uphold an alternate version of oneself, so one's true self isn't discovered. This list could go on.

When these parts show up in us, we innately try to shut them down. We certainly don't view the feelings that accompany these parts as good. They seem to be "in the way." They create more trouble. And the cultural solution is often to make them your enemy, fix the feelings, or get rid of them quickly. This is what I did for so long in my own life. When my trembling and anxiety showed up, I viewed them as unwanted and wrong and worked to resolve or rid myself of them ASAP. This approach didn't bring me relief, but I didn't know any other solution back then.

DITCHING THE SHOULDS

Something began to change when I started dating that first woman when I was thirty-five. I found myself questioning, in a new way, whose rules I wanted to follow: my own or those placed on me from the outside. A new curiosity slowly bloomed that allowed for micro-moment pauses and invited me to notice what felt truly aligned and authentic for *me on the inside*. More and more, I began to notice how I was living my life and what I was doing that felt aligned for me and what I was doing because I thought I *should*.

That was a big moment, friends. And it might be for you too. Whether it's related to your relationship, job, place of residence, friends, or something else, are you in the situation because you want to be or because you think you should be? If you feel you have no choice, pause and see whether you think you *should* stay in it because you believe you're expected to.

Can you feel how "shoulds" shut us down? They cut us off from letting ourselves dream bigger or beyond where we are. They convince us that it's not acceptable to have what we want or to follow the trail of nudges guiding us to new aspects of ourselves. They inhibit our connection with our inner compass, God, or the Universe, leaving our focus dependent upon outside expectations for our life. "Shoulds" place our entire focus outside ourselves. This doesn't feel good, and it's not supposed to! When our day-to-day choices are based upon others' expectations of us, whether personal or societal, this cuts us off from ourselves.

I learned this when I started dating the woman who would one day become my wife. Something in me relaxed. I felt more like myself than ever. And rather than worrying that my girlfriend news would go against the expectations my cousins held for me, my focus was on sharing with them something I knew to be aligned for me on the inside of my soul. Instead of wondering if I was doing things the "right" way, I *knew* I was because it didn't feel like a should. It felt like a *yes*.

And when I shared with my cousins that I had a girlfriend, my thirty-plus years of church trembles vanished the following day! They were simply gone.

At first, I was puzzled by this. But over time, I've come to understand that I took ownership of my expectations for my life that night. I laid down others' expectations, whether real or imagined, and declared that my own counted the most. And just like that, my shaking no longer needed to be the messenger trying to call me back home to myself.

While "shoulds" don't own me the way they did for so long, they still show up in my life because they're part of our human journey. And contrary to what our thinking minds often believe, it's freeing to discover where the shoulds are showing up in our present moments. It allows us to explore what the shoulds are, as well as our authentic desires that are being inhibited by these shoulds. The process invites us back home.

One particular should that still shows up for me sometimes is giving myself a label now that I have a wife. People like to know what box others fit into. Many assume I'm gay now that I have a wife. And in truth, I often call myself gay when speaking with others because it simplifies things. But if I'm honest, what I am doesn't have a name. And I like that. I recently had a conversation with a lesbian friend. I told her I had stick-straight hair until I "went" gay, at which point my hair developed waves and curls that I'd always been convinced were stuck inside my head! She laughed and challenged my use of the phrase "went gay," suggesting that wasn't genuinely accurate, assuming I'd always been gay. But I spent thirty-five years living and breathing as a heterosexual as far as I knew. And then that moment came when I fell in love with a woman. It was a turning point. It marked a before and after for me. Before that point, I'd navigated life from the outside in, always trying to figure out how to be according to outside expectations.

But from that point onward, I began to navigate life from a different vantage point inside myself. That was the moment when I began to come home to myself. I felt freedom to be me as the limiting boxes fell away. I experienced a sense of space I hadn't known I was missing. At the same time, I repeatedly discover another expectation on the other side of this that demands I update my label and name it. And yet my insides now rebel when I give myself a label. In truth,

I've learned that a billion different roads carry each of us into our awareness of identity and sexuality. And sometimes, we can only see one or two possibilities until something comes along and creates unexpected space for us. Then we can tap into new truths inside ourselves that were always there but never before known. And that's where I find myself. In the space. Without the labels. In love with my wife. Having spent so many years trying to fit into boxes and meet the external shoulds reflected all around me, there is an incredible freedom that comes with sitting in this space, simply being me.

Some may read this chapter and feel pressured to don a lens of wrongness and get to work, rooting out all the "wrong" shoulds in your life. If this is you, I invite you to pause. Attempting to get to the bottom of all the shoulds will keep you on an endless hamster wheel and pin your lens of wrongness in place. We'll always be able to find more shoulds in our lives. It's not about eradicating them. It's about *curiously* noticing the ones showing up in *this* moment of your life. Those are the ones impacting you now. These are the ones asking to be seen by you. And coming to know them with a lens of curiosity rather than wrongness can transform your now too.

Some *Power Questions* (more on these in chapter eight) that can be helpful to ask as you explore this for yourself:

- What if it turns out that as I let go of the shoulds in my life, I'll feel more and more at home in myself?

- I wonder what I'll discover I *want* to do if I let go of what I'm convinced I *should* do?

Where are the shoulds showing up in your life right now? If you could let go of the shoulds and outside expectations, what would you want to do, and how would you want to feel? What are your authentic desires hidden behind those shoulds? This is your one wondrous life. And you get to make the rules and define your *own* expectations. What will they be?

Chapter Six

AND THEN THE GOD GANG WAS BORN

Every week, I sat in those church pews, feeling short of breath. Remember, I'm a P. K. (preacher's kid), so I spent many a Sunday in those pews! I experienced this shortness of breath at church for as long as I can remember. And like clockwork, it resolved once I got home each Sunday. At some point, I concluded there must be mold in the church I grew up in, causing a reaction in my lungs. And that's the explanation I landed on for many years. But as I grew older and moved away from home, I noticed it happened in other churches too. When I went to the little Episcopal church on Fire Island each summer, that shortness of breath was always waiting for me. I experienced it in churches all over the United States and overseas.

Curiosity about my episodic, church-related shortness of breath increased over time. I never considered that my shortness of breath was a messenger. Instead, I brushed these symptoms aside and repeatedly searched for a church to make my own. I didn't want to disappoint my parents. My mom mentioned numerous times that it made my dad sad when I didn't attend church. And remember, for eons, outside expectations were what I knew to follow. I hadn't yet stepped into my ability to navigate my life from the inside, so I tried to figure out the church thing by meeting outside familial expectations. And in truth, because I'm a P. K., I assumed others held this expectation for me, too, whether they actually did or not.

People-pleasing can be so insidious. I was not one bit aware that my goal of finding a church had anything to do with making *others* happy. I also didn't realize I wasn't taking my feelings into account. This is another experience in which my lens of wrongness was incredibly present, but I didn't know it. That lens had me trying to figure out how to do the "right" thing according to outside expectations of others, whether real or imagined. It had me convinced there *was* even a right way to handle church. It also left me certain that my church-related shortness of breath was a meaningless symptom.

But I forgot to consult myself during these years. That lens of wrongness held my focus outside of me. It cut me off not only from myself but from curiosity. That's exactly what a lens of wrongness does when we're in the midst of it. And that's where I remained for many years of my thirties, repeatedly attempting to find a church, followed by momentary breaks from the search before the guilt grew big enough that my search resumed. All the while, that shortness of breath at church followed me.

It was in my forties that I began to learn how to harness curiosity in my life, which slowly began to soften my experience with this lens of wrongness. Remember, curiosity is the antidote. A lens of wrongness requires black-and-white, all-or-nothing thinking. Something is either right or wrong. There's no middle ground. But curiosity? That changes everything because it removes the boxes we so easily construct. It invites us to look beyond the labels to which we've been so convincingly tied. More space is created for us to notice how we feel in response to an experience, an idea, or even a label or box with which we've identified for so long.

New Questions

My newer curiosity led me to ask questions I'd never considered. Questions about God, church, religion, and my beliefs. I wondered what my beliefs were and whether I felt aligned with these beliefs I'd assumed for most of my life. Maybe you know this place, whether it's about religion or something else. How often do we carry beliefs handed down from our families, culture, religious institutions, social circles, etc.? We frequently don't even pause and wonder about these beliefs. We simply move through life, assuming they're ours too. I certainly experienced this when I dated a woman for the first time at thirty-five. I'd so definitively believed I was solely heterosexual. And all at once, those beliefs were challenged when my experience invited curiosity. I considered what felt truly aligned with me on the inside, separate from outside expectations and others' beliefs. This is the same process I experienced around God and church when curiosity came on the scene.

Just as it was disorienting for me when I first began to question my beliefs about my sexuality, it was equally disorienting as space opened up for me to consider my own beliefs about God. I learned that this disorientation can be an important part of coming home to ourselves honestly and authentically, but I can't say I loved it in the moment. As I moved through this time, I began to feel far away from God, which was disconcerting, as I'd always felt a connection before this time. I found myself wondering if God even existed. I walked through my days doubting his presence more and more and noticing how notably different and meaningless my life felt without God in it. Yet my doubt of his existence only grew. As I considered the possibility of no God and no afterlife, I felt increasingly empty. Connection to others is an integral part of who I am, and losing a belief in an afterlife left me feeling even more disconnected from those I've loved dearly who are no longer physically alive.

It made me relate to others who move through life without believing in something greater than themselves. It made me grateful that I was only discovering this "truth" in my forties rather than from the start of my life, because I was left empty and disconnected. This was not an experience I'd ever expected to have, and it felt so distressing. Perhaps some of you know this experience yourselves. My lens of wrongness had me convinced that there was either a God or no God, that God was the way I'd always known him or no way.

As I walked my dog one particularly cold winter afternoon, I felt the emptiness in my chest. I was overwhelmed by a grief-filled disappointment as I concluded that I'd been mistaken all these years, believing in a God who didn't exist. I felt let down and incredibly alone. Up to that point, I hadn't spoken my updated beliefs aloud, but I heard myself saying to the wind around me, "God, I can't believe I thought you existed all this time when I was just talking to nothing. This new reality fucking sucks." And that's when I heard it. First, one voice, then another, and another. Jesus said, "Well, I'm here!" God exclaimed, "I've been here the whole time, honey." Mohammed said, "Me too." Buddha confirmed his presence. And then others I didn't know also confirmed their presence. And because these voices threw me for a loop, I looked around to see where they were coming from. But another part of me knew I wouldn't find them because I could feel their presence inside my chest. That may sound odd or even crazy, but it's true. My chest felt warm despite the cold air I was sucking in, and butterflies filled my stomach as wonder and curiosity took over.

In those few moments, my God Gang (GG) was born. In an instant, I knew less about God than ever before, yet also felt a personal, direct presence and connection that was simultaneously foreign and profoundly familiar. I tentatively asked them what was going on, feeling silly and even wondering if I was experiencing a psychotic episode. But they were quick to respond, letting me know they'd always been with me. I told them I was reluctant to believe it. They made it clear they had no problem with my reluctance and doubt. There was no pressure for me to understand or believe. I experienced only a sense of excitement from them as they seemed simply thrilled to be connecting with me in this way. As I walked home after this most surprising interaction, I felt different, as if something inside me had realigned in a way I'd never before experienced.

I expected my interactions with this brand-new GG to fade. I assumed it was one of those unexplainable moments of meaning that would quickly become a memory. But that's not what happened. This gang kept showing up! I had a longtime habit of walking the dog and reviewing whatever was stressing me out on a given day. This habit continued, but suddenly the GG was piping in to offer their insight on my latest anxiety, stressor, or conundrum. Their words were always reassuring, soothing, and loving.

DEAD TREE LESSONS

A short time into my relationship with the GG, a situation with a neighbor and a dead tree arose. A tree adjacent to our property began dropping large, dead limbs onto our driveway where we frequently parked the car and walked with our kids. I called the landlord and owner of the house next door to let her know. When she came to look at the tree, she told me it was on my property. We discussed it, and I shared my understanding that it was on her property. She said she would investigate the property lines and get back to me.

Then two months went by. Limbs continued to drop, so we stopped accessing the driveway. Each time I called her, she ignored my calls or said she was still working on it. I became increasingly angry and started "going all New York" on her. I mean, I *am* from New York, and I *know* how to be fiery and assertive when I need to be! She would stop by her house next door, and we would argue. I would push back, clearly stating the need for the tree to come down. Then I would go inside and realize that as good as I was at "going all New York," I was always left shaking, with my heart racing furiously.

My mind was *consumed* with figuring out how to fix this issue. I lost sleep over it. I stressed over it. And I constantly planned what my next steps of action would be.

And then, one morning, I woke up and heard the GG say, "Wait another day, honey." I was annoyed, but I was also a little curious because it was a different approach from the one I'd been taking that was getting me nowhere.

I waited another day. I woke up the next day and heard the same damn thing. I was annoyed again but still curious, so I waited some more. This daily message to wait went on for nearly two weeks. A part of me continued to argue against this approach. At the end of those weeks, I was leaving my office for the day and thought to myself, "That's it. I'm *not* waiting *any longer*. I'm going home to take action!"

I drove home, got out of my car, and nearly fell over. The surveyor had come while I was at work and marked all the property lines. The tree in question sat clearly on our neighbor's property. And within five days, the tree was taken down. This "wait one more day" quietly brought me back into the present moment, so I took things one day at a time during a frustrating experience of powerlessness. This created space in me. It loosened my grip on the unknowns about which I was trying to feel in control. It made more room in my brain because I was spending less active time worrying. And the solutions showed up with more ease. It turned out I didn't need to spend so much energy trying to figure it all out and make it happen because solutions were being worked out under the surface that I couldn't yet see. Needless to say, this experience certainly grew my trust in the GG and their guidance.

WHEN CURIOSITY AND GOD COLLIDE

After a few months of these almost daily interactions with the GG, I realized there were no women in the gang, which began to bother me. I let the GG know this. About two weeks later, a new member of the GG presented herself. And she took me by surprise. She's a butchy lesbian GG member who has yet to reveal her name. She's incredibly loving and caring and became the main GG member who showed up for me over that next year. More recently, a wise, heavyset Black woman has made herself known to me. She goes by Clarice. She's direct and honest with me, even when it's something I don't want to hear, but does so in a deeply loving and reassuring way that repeatedly soothes my soul. And she calls me "baby girl." As you can see, the GG continues to challenge the boxes and labels I'd learned to use to define God. At one point, I asked God about these other GG members, and God said, "Honey, they are all faces of mine. It's whoever you're needing at a given time." Talk about a spacious experience of God.

Something I've noticed is that when I use the term *God*, I'm only able to associate the term with the male gender. My mind only knows how to refer to God simultaneously with he/him. But if I'm honest, my experience of God is often not gendered, which is why I love my newfound freedom to have different faces of God show up in the GG, depending on what I need at that moment.

What I've gone on to understand is that my church-related shortness of breath was *never* wrong, and it certainly wasn't meaningless; it was simply a messenger. It wasn't a reaction to mold. My body communicated a desire for more spaciousness around the labels and boxes I experienced in church. Were these boxes a direct result of my dad being a priest? This may be a surprise, but I don't believe so. My dad is a notably progressive, open thinker regarding religion. We didn't grow up believing in the devil or even the possibility of going to hell after death. It wasn't part of our family construct to believe that only those who believe in Jesus Christ can go to heaven. Our world is made up of so many different people with differing beliefs and faiths. When a lens of wrongness is applied to religion, it becomes tempting to use black-and-white, all-or-nothing thinking to believe that one faith is better than the others. This is why curiosity is the antidote to the rigidity accompanying a lens of wrongness, even when it comes to religion.

One of the more profound understandings I've stepped into since meeting the GG is that God shows up to us in many ways, using a myriad of faces. For some, it's Jesus. For others, it's Mohammed, Buddha, the Divine, Spirit, the Divine Mother, Angel Guides, or the Universe. Maybe the face is Nature herself or something else altogether. For me, sometimes it's my loving, butchy lesbian GG member; my direct, reassuring Black GG member named Clarice; an orange butterfly; a white dog; or God. I'm always interested when a new GG member makes itself known to me. I appreciate the spaciousness I feel around my sense of God now. And I appreciate being able to ask for what I need, even when I want more female or non-binary members in the God Gang.

What I've come to understand is that my relationship with the church was complicated after my experience with sexual abuse and the secrecy that followed when I was five. Tied into my relationship with God and church was a belief that I had to have one version of myself on the outside that I showed to others while a different version of me lived on the inside. The inside version held the secret of my sexual abuse, which resulted in a belief that I must be wrong or bad, or it wouldn't need to be a secret. It taught me that I couldn't let others see my badness. When I recognize this, my church-related shortness of breath makes sense. It's as if the inside version of me was trying to breathe as shallowly as possible in the hope that she would not be detected. She was trying to live within the lines, boxes, and labels she perceived through her lens of wrongness. And it was suffocating her.

But she's no longer suffocating. She freely fills her lungs with air. She's slipped from a lens of wrongness into curiosity. She now knows her feelings matter and that they always did. She revels in her spaciousness as she explores what feels truest for her, what feels aligned and what kind of a relationship she wants with God and the GG. And so do I.

This chapter was hard for me to write. It took me over six months to write more than a few lines. I felt confused. I was scared to talk about God for all to read. I was afraid I would do it wrong or that my words would turn some away. And in truth, maybe they have. But it all changed when I realized how profoundly our human lens of wrongness impacts our relationship with a higher power of our understanding. All over the media, we see evidence of this. The black-and-white, all-or-nothing, rigid thinking that comes with a lens of wrongness. The belief that God only does relationships in one particular way, that God is definitively male, that we have to believe or do church or religion or spirituality in specific ways to have, earn, or keep God's love.

I've worked with many patients over the last few years who have lost their faith in something bigger than themselves despite growing up religious. And most of them are distressed by this. They describe feeling disoriented and angry. And they frequently feel more alone. I've been so grateful for the GG and my updated beliefs, and I love sharing this with my patients because it's freeing for them to discover that their doubts haven't been wrong! I regularly suggest that their doubts simply invite them to step into curiosity and consider what kind of a relationship they *want* with a higher power of their understanding. What if it isn't about doing church or God or religion in a particular, "right" way but is instead about doing it in a way that feels true and aligned to each of us? What face or version of God works best for you?

I hope to be around for many years to come. And I trust that my understanding of and relationship with God and the God Gang (and whoever else comes along!) and even church will continue to evolve. I don't know what it will look or feel like as time passes. What I do know is that it feels deliciously spacious to be able to approach this journey with curiosity. Remember, when we shift into curiosity, this allows us to step beyond the limiting options that a lens of wrongness offers. What if it turns out there's *not* only one right way to be a Christian, Jew, Muslim, Hindu, agnostic, or even atheist? What if attending a place of worship is a perfect fit for some, while others find their connection to God or a higher power of their understanding outside the confines of a building? When we step beyond the lens of wrongness and into curiosity, all these become equally beautiful options instead of wrong ones. I wonder where this curiosity will lead each of us in the future?

Chapter Seven

HOW TO LOWER THE BAR AND FINALLY SUCCEED IN SELF-CARE

Let's talk about what it was like to be around me whenever I prepared for guests to visit, specifically *before* I learned how to come back home to myself. Before I met my wife, my cleaning frenzies were simply something I did. I'd wait until twelve to twenty-four hours before guests arrived to start cleaning and organizing. I'd throw myself into this job no matter what was going on for me. It didn't matter if I had a migraine, the flu, or hadn't slept in three days; I still cleaned. It also didn't matter if I was starving, needed to pee, or was exhausted. I disregarded it all and kept going.

And then my wife and I moved in together. I continued to have these cleaning frenzies, but now I had someone around me who didn't view my behavior the same way I did. She didn't give me accolades for it. She worried about me instead. She said, "Honey, maybe you should take a break. Our guests aren't gonna care whether the house is perfect. You haven't eaten in a long time. Why don't you drink some water and eat or just sit down for a few minutes?"

Well, you'd think I would appreciate her thoughtful interventions, but they utterly pissed me off! She was getting in the way of me accomplishing what I needed to do to get the house perfect. Her lack of worry about the house being perfect further convinced me that she just didn't get it, which meant I was on my own with the responsibility of preparing the house. I can't begin to tell you how many patients and friends I have shared this scenario with over the years who were shocked to learn they aren't the only ones with this particular pre-guest frenzy style.

That scenario describes how impossible it felt for me to include self-care when preparing for the arrival of guests. But the truth is that this tended to be how I felt about doing self-care in any part of my life. There simply wasn't time for it. I needed to keep accomplishing, getting things done, checking things off my never-ending to-do list, and taking care of others' needs. There wasn't any time left for self-care. Have you ever noticed how quietly self-care demands can become yet another obligation in your life? And before you know it, your inner bully is criticizing you even more because you failed, yet again, to succeed in your self-care attempts. It's such an exhausting cycle.

In college, I often daydreamed about my future life as an adult. It always included this one particular scenario: spending weekend mornings reading the newspaper next to my husband while sipping coffee. But I've never been a coffee drinker, I ended up with a wife, and rarely have I used the newspaper to access my news!

Here's another thing I've loved to daydream about for as long as I can remember: climbing into my bed early in the evening to spend time reading, journaling, meditating, or praying. But that's not how it turned out for a long time. Sometimes I'd get sucked into a TV show my wife was watching. Or I'd easily find more work that needed to be done. Or when I finished that, I'd open social media for a "quick" scroll, and we all know how that goes.

There was a running joke in my beloved "framily" (friends who are like family) with whom I lived in Australia in my early thirties. In the later evenings, I stood behind the couch while they watched TV. Yes, I watched it, too, but I never sat down. They laughed and encouraged me to sit, but I always refused. If I sat down, it meant I was concretely deciding not to have my time upstairs by myself, which is something I always craved. However, most often this meant that I spent countless hours watching TV while standing, never quite making it up those stairs to my bedroom for that coveted self-time.

RELENTLESS SELF-IMPROVEMENT PROJECT

For my first forty years, doing and accomplishing was my absolute default mode. This is a mode that runs many of our lives. Something strange happens when we're in the default mode of doing and accomplishing. We more easily lose touch with ourselves. I'll bet you can notice this even if you've never thought about it before. The faster you try to meet all the expectations you've put on yourself, and check off all the boxes in life, the more it feels necessary to disregard your own needs. In fact, you probably don't even realize you're doing it because it simply feels like there's no room for your needs. It often feels like no one else is making room for them either

Do you know what else happens when we throw ourselves into the busy doing and accomplishing mode and put everyone else's needs before our own? Our bodies start to communicate with us. And what starts as a whisper soon becomes a yell. On the surface, it simply looks like the body is struggling due to the increased stress. It can even feel like your body is betraying you as your health declines in any number of ways. That was certainly my experience when I navigated chronic illness in my twenties and again in my thirties. And then you search for how to fix your body that feels increasingly broken.

But we *all* know what it feels like to discover yet another thing in our lives that feels so wrong and needs to be fixed.

It's damn exhausting. It can leave you feeling like a relentless self-improvement project. You start by realizing that you are once again so busy and so stressed. You make that decision for the millionth time to do better with your self-care You throw yourself into it. And maybe you pull it off successfully for a week. Or maybe two. But then the demands of self-care become one more expectation on your plate. And you start to resent the acts of self-care altogether. And before you know it, you're once again drowning in your busyness and stress. But now your inner bully is criticizing you even more because you failed, yet again, to succeed in self-care. And there's that wrongness again, but this time it's around how bad you are at self-care. Argh!

What if I told you there's an easier way to shift some of those self-care struggles? What if it doesn't require that you become a relentless self-improvement project, working hard to make the changes happen, but instead invites you to come home to yourself in the micro-moments again? It turns out this is true. My patients who have played with this approach agree, finding it removes their inner battle to master the self-care gig.

Can you think of an area in your life where self-care feels impossible? Are you ready to put down the relentless guilt about not practicing self-care well enough and try a different way?

A Surprising Way to Make Self-Care Easier

Let's go back to my earlier story of yearning to get into bed early each evening to read but having a *really* hard time making it happen. For many years, I'd go through phases of trying to *force* myself to do this act of self-care. As often happens, this kind of change lasts for a short time but then peters out. It's too big a jump from one action to the other, *and* only your mind is driving it.

But you know what changed my experience with this? When I lowered the bar. Yup. I changed my expectations. The *only* thing I asked myself to do was to notice what it *felt* like in my body as I chose to stay downstairs when I wanted to be climbing into bed. And I only asked myself to notice this for micro-moments. That's it.

Why is this powerful? Because it invites you home inside yourself. It drops your focus from up in the attic of your mind, down into your body. It is the opposite of disregarding yourself or making your symptoms wrong. It's saying to your body, "I'm tuning in to you. I can feel my resentment toward whomever or whatever is 'keeping' me from doing what I really want to be doing. My chest or shoulders feel heavy. I feel agitated, etc."

I also began to apply this to my pre-guest cleaning frenzies. At first, this didn't look like much. I paused for a second or two to notice what it felt like in my body while frantically cleaning. I discovered it felt *terrible* in there, which was unexpected for me because I was accustomed to checking *out* of my body during my cleaning rampages.

At first, I could only pause to notice this for those one to two seconds before the pressure to resume cleaning became too big and I had to step back into the frenzy. But over time, those seconds turned into thirty seconds in which I would lie flat on the bed or floor and notice what was happening inside me. I was startled to find that those thirty seconds felt like a relief to me even though I also noticed my heart was pounding; my blood felt like it was racing through my body like a wild, chaotic ocean current; and my mind was running in a million different directions, landing on no thought and many thoughts all at once. These micro-moment breaks suspended my lens of wrongness and made me curious about my internal experience.

As I continued to practice this, more unexpected side effects occurred. Those thirty-second breaks brought me back home to me, and I started to more easily notice if I was hungry, thirsty, tired, or needed to pee. The thirty seconds turned into five-minute breaks, which turned into thirty-minute breaks as I continued to practice this over time. It became possible for me to pause and feed myself, use the loo, hydrate, or take a break

I found myself asking an outlandishly new question: *why* did the house need to be perfect for my guests in the first place? Once again, these micro-moment pauses to come back home to me in the middle of my unwanted feelings or experiences created space for me to discover that nothing outside me had ever needed to be fixed to make me more right, acceptable, or lovable on the inside. I'd never been innately wrong or broken in the first place.

Believe it or not, practicing this regularly, when you remember to, begins to embolden the *why* that's driving your ability to make new choices. The more you notice how uncomfortable it feels inside when you're in a cleaning frenzy, getting sucked into another TV show, scrolling more on social media, eating bags of cookies on the couch, working late into the night on your laptop, or running around like a chicken with your head cut off as you try to meet everyone else's needs, well, the more you naturally create presence within yourself in these micro-moments. And this presence increases your ability not only to recognize but *own* that how you feel *does* matter. It counts. And you count. A cool side effect of this? Your body will begin to show you an appreciation for these moments. You don't even have to make outward changes in your self-care behavior to begin to feel a difference in your body.

Practicing these micro-moments of tuning in *is* a form of self-care! And after a little bit of practice, even for seconds at a time, new neural pathways begin to form in your noggin, showing your mind a different way to navigate those times when you feel burned out, untended to, or simply over-committed. And it starts with coming *home* to ourselves in those moments when our minds want to take us *outside* ourselves to search for the fastest way to fix or numb how we're feeling.

This doesn't mean I never slide into a pre-guest cleaning

frenzy anymore, or that I now go to bed early every night! It means that I *still* get on a roll of moving too fast and doing too much and start disregarding myself. But my tolerance for what that feels like inside me has changed. I notice those uncomfortable feelings so much more quickly. And those newer neural pathways remind my brain and me that it's time to come back home and be present with my experience on the inside. This ultimately makes it more possible for me to change my behavior in a direction that serves me better and honors just how much my needs count in my world too.

What about you? What's that thing in your life that you crave, yet the busyness of life or others' needs repeatedly draw you farther from it? Are you ready to suspend your lens of wrongness, put down the relentless guilt about not practicing self-care well enough, and try it differently? The next time you find yourself doing that thing when you *really* wish you were doing that other thing that truly feeds your soul, *pause* in that micro-moment. Invite your focus inside and drop it down from the attic of your mind and into your body. Notice what it feels like inside when you're doing something that takes you away from what you're really needing. *There's no need to try to fix it.* Simply notice. And then go on with things. When you think of it again, drop inside and notice again. Each second or so that you do this, you are further building that new neural pathway that makes outer changes in your self-care behavior easier and more possible over time. And just like that, your days of feeling like a failure at self-care and like a relentless self-improvement project are no longer needed in the way they once were.

Chapter Eight

LOOKING FOR ANSWERS IN ALL THE WRONG PLACES

I remember a particular young patient I worked with almost thirty years ago. We crossed paths after she sustained a complex fracture at the hands of her husband. I'll leave out the details of how this occurred, but I assure you it was horrific. Before this, her life had been filled with a mixture of good times and abuse, but it was a life she knew well. Everything changed after this incident because she knew she couldn't return to her husband. She'd reached her point of no return. She was brave. And she was filled with anxiety about the uncertainty ahead of her. She felt paralyzed by it.

I know this place too. When I fell in love with a woman that first time, the life I'd come to count on felt so confusing. I was uncertain about my identity in a way I'd never experienced. My mind future-tripped like crazy about everything I was scared might happen, imagining others' reactions when I shared my news with them. I was even worried about what strangers in my future might think about me one day!

When anxious and uncertain, you're naturally drawn outside yourself to find the answers. There's a feeling of desperation that often begins to accompany the unknown. An inner pressure builds, pushing you to hurry up and find a way back to certainty. Reflecting on this painfully uncertain period in my life, I noticed a few interesting things. For one, my mind was repeatedly hell-bent on leading me back into future-tripping mode because it was convinced the certainty would be found there. Instead, it consistently led me away from certainty.

But whenever I tapped back into the present and my inner compass, clarity about the next steps came. I never found this clarity when I followed the desperate inner pressure to get myself back to certainty quickly. Instead, when I rested in the present moment, the small knowings showed up. They didn't surface as one big knowing that fixed everything. Instead, they came in small bites. Each of these steps guided me through my fear and uncertainty. They ultimately led me to a life that has far surpassed my expectations.

Uncertainty undoubtedly swirls around you sometimes as you steer your way through life. Maybe it's your work that feels so uncertain. Perhaps it's your finances, your home, your kids, your relationships, your health, or any number of other unknowns. You likely feel that call of desperation that follows uncertainty. It pushes you to search anxiously outside yourself for the next steps that will lead you back to certainty.

But what if your next steps are perched *inside* you rather than somewhere out there? What if purposely tuning into the meaningful parts of this present moment will reconnect you with your inner compass? What if this connection clarifies the next steps in small, digestible portions? And what if each of these small steps carries you more toward solutions and the relief your mind has been anxiously trying to find? This is true. And I know there is no better time than now to discover this for yourself.

Two years after working with her, I ran into the patient I mentioned. She looked like a different person as she stood there, sparkling with joy. She said, "Do you remember me? You helped me two years ago. When we finished working together, I bought a small plant because you told me I was like a flowering plant that hadn't been watered or cared for in a long time. You said it was time for me to water and tend to my own plant. You said this would allow me to bloom.

"I was so scared at first. Everything in my life was so uncertain. But tending to that plant reminded me to tend to myself too. I could only handle a day at a time for a long while, but this made me more present – some of the time, anyway. And each day, I took the next step that felt clear.

"And guess what happened? I bloomed! I returned to school, got my degree, and now I have a great job. Every time I look at that plant, it reminds me to connect with myself and how that's allowed me to bloom *through* my fear and uncertainty!"

If you are someone who periodically finds yourself surfing anxiety and uncertainty like the rest of us humans do, I remind you that we are ALL flowering plants that need tending. When you catch yourself future-tripping and anxiously searching for solutions, I invite you to play with stepping back into your present moments. This is a surefire way to tend to yourself.

Micro-moment pauses enable us to notice the meaningful moments we're having, whether in our relationships, in nature, in our home, or with something else altogether. This reconnects us with our inner compass and those quiet, little knowings that slip into our awareness and offer clarity. We then know the next steps we can take during uncertain times, so we can move toward relief more easily. The good news is that there are simple tools we can apply to the present moments that help us to usher in this clarity with more ease.

HARD I DON'T KNOWS VERSUS SOFT I DON'T KNOWS

In the first months of the COVID pandemic, the isolation felt somewhat manageable. Quarantining was new and different.

The slower pace was even a relief. The time with family felt nourishing. But somewhere between weeks five and six, something began to feel different. My tolerance to stress decreased. My normal ability to multitask waned. My anxiety increased.

Without realizing it, I kicked into using what I call a *Hard I Don't Know*, which is an old-time default of mine when I'm facing the unknown and it automatically uses a lens of wrongness. Maybe you'll recognize this approach. You're not sure what will happen, so you start stressing about what *could* happen. In the presence of uncertainty, your thinking mind goes into overdrive, trying to find the answers. You work harder and harder and with great intensity to find the solutions. Your mind identifies more things to worry about, and then it works like a hellion to figure out how to fix them. You feel desperate to uncover some way to gain even a small sense of control in an uncertain situation.

Yeah. The *Hard I Don't Knows* never feel good, and they always make us feel so gripped with stress. But sometimes we have to hang out in that place for a bit. The tricky part is that when I'm in a *Hard I Don't Know*, I feel increasingly anxious and I become convinced all the responsibility to fix things lies solely on my shoulders.

I periodically consider turning this stuff over to God or my GG when I'm in this mode. And sometimes I do, but my jaw usually tenses, my hands clench, and my muscles tighten as my mind yells, "OK, God, what the hell am I supposed to *do*? Huh? Where are the solutions?" And as soon as I finish saying this, I turn back around, pick up all my worries, and start hauling them around again, searching for the fixes. And it feels terrible.

Has a *Hard I Don't Know* ever owned you? It often leaves you with growing anxiety and a sense of urgency to find the answers to an ever-increasing array of worries and uncertainties. The more you look around, the more things you notice wrong in your life and the more worries you find.

Early in the pandemic, I sat in this *Hard I Don't Know* for a challenging, uncomfortable few weeks before I found myself thinking about other times of uncertainty in my life. There have been so many experiences when uncertainty ruled and then clarity moved in, or when solutions felt impossible and then new answers not on my radar showed up. Many times were smaller moments, but some were bigger like that first time I fell in love with a woman, and when I was diagnosed with cancer. You may also remember my story about my neighbor and the dead tree.

You can think of times like this in your own life. Times when uncertainty was present, overwhelming, and sometimes even paralyzing. Solutions felt impossible or limited and unhelpful, which only made your anxious mind spin more. And then answers showed up. Creative solutions unexpectedly plopped into your mind. A random conversation with someone unexpectedly allowed new perspectives to sneak in with a different angle on the uncertain situation. Solutions you'd never seen coming materialized.

The pressure and anxiety I'd felt softened as I remembered these times of uncertainty that ultimately worked out, often in ways far better than I had envisioned. Hope reawakened in me. This enabled me to quietly shift from a *Hard I Don't Know* to a *Soft I Don't Know*, which is very different. A *Soft I Don't Know* doesn't have any fight. It doesn't feel desperate. Instead, it feels curious. Notice how this naturally shifts us from a lens of wrongness to one of curiosity.

I always appreciate when a *Soft I Don't Know* sneaks in. Or when I remember to invite it in. Instead of demanding that I find a solution to the uncertainty, curiosity takes over. My hands move from clenched to a soft, open, questioning position as I ask myself, "Huh. I wonder how this is all going to work out? I wonder what solutions will show up that I haven't even thought of yet?" And just like that, my body lets go a bit. My jaw loosens, and my shoulders drop down from my ears.

As the *Soft I Don't Know* slid in, I became more open to writing letters to H. P. in the mornings. That's the nickname I've used to write to God over the years. It's short for Higher Power, and H. P. is often my chummy, casual term when I'm not writing to God or the God Gang. *Morning H. P. Well, all I know is that the weight of stress I'm carrying on my shoulders, the uncertainty, and the number of things I'm convinced I need to fix feel way too heavy. I'm just gonna surrender them to this journal and you and let them go for the day. Huh. I wonder how things will turn out?*

I did this the next day. And the next. Each day I turned over whatever was stressing me, even the little stuff. I surrendered it *all* to the pages of that journal and H. P. and then went on with my day feeling a bit lighter. And I felt relief. My shoulders became lighter. I started laughing again. It became easier to be present without working so hard at it. My mind relaxed even though all the solutions weren't yet here. As I practiced this *Soft I Don't Know*, my curiosity about the solutions grew while my anxiety and sense of responsibility to find all the fixes dissipated. In fact, my list of worries grew shorter even though uncertainty remained. It was no longer necessary to get rid of all my stressors or solve all my worries to find relief because my reactions to them softened.

When you move into a *Soft I Don't Know*, a lens of curiosity begins to lead you rather than a lens of wrongness. It creates space and time for possibilities rather than demanding solutions before the timing is right. And it invites you to purposefully identify the things causing you stress and turn them over to something other than yourself and your ever-willing-to-work mind. If you have a belief in something bigger than yourself, great! But if you don't, that's OK too. This isn't about forcing you to believe in something that doesn't feel authentic. This is about finding a way to lighten the load on your shoulders.

During times of uncertainty, I invite you to purposely notice the times in your life when periods of uncertainty ultimately *did* turn out well for you. Couple that with taking action to identify and then dump those stressors and worries in a journal, on a higher power of your understanding, or both. And then *leave them there for the day.* Give yourself a break from the worry of having to solve problems or fix them. Just for the day. Or even for a few hours.

It's helpful to remember that when worries and anxieties abound, your mind often tries to convince you that putting more time and effort into finding the solutions will finally bring relief. But what if it turns out that finding ways to put those worries down, even for a few minutes or hours, creates space for solutions to slip in more easily? Again and again, I find this to be true, and you just might too. It sure is helpful to remember that the *Soft I Don't Knows* are waiting for us when we're ready. We can unclench our hands, even for a moment, and wonder what solutions will show up that we haven't even thought of yet. What unknowns in *your* life could use a *Soft I Don't Know* right about now?

FINDING FRESH PERSPECTIVE
IN THE CHALLENGING MOMENTS

Sometimes, kiddos remind us of what's true.

My wife and I went on a daytime date about six months into the pandemic. We left the kids home with our beloved babysitter for another COVID-style afternoon of outdoor babysitting. They went hiking in the woods and returned home just as the skies opened. This meant they were confined to the covered front porch for "arting" and games.

When we returned from our date, we found our nine-year-old reading, but how she was reading surprised us. She'd moved a small wooden chair off the porch and onto the pathway that leads to the street. She'd maneuvered a ladybug umbrella so that it covered most of her body while she sat in the chair reading in the rain. It totally cracked us up, but it also reminded me of something. There are many ways to view our challenging circumstances even when it doesn't always feel this way!

Having to stay on the front porch due to the rain could have left her feeling trapped. But instead, she thought outside the box. The rain didn't mean her options were limited. And she clearly remembered this. But how often do we remember this as adults? The onset of the pandemic in 2020 surely created a feeling of limits and decreased options, but it also invited us to think outside the box. I saw this happening everywhere. Creative ways of schooling, new ways of dining out, brand-new ways of socializing and connecting, etc.

Despite our marked limitations, new options and perspectives were always perched, just waiting to be discovered. Our thinking minds often forget this, though. They become convinced of the limitations, only seeing what's wrong, which can't help but affect our mood. I've learned it feels impossible to view my challenging circumstances in empowering ways when my thinking mind has me convinced there aren't any other perspectives available.

There's a trick that's often helpful in these moments. We can phrase questions in a certain way and pose them to our thinking minds without expecting an answer. It's a way to give our minds something to chew on. And in that process, our thinking mind unintentionally becomes curious! These questions usher in a lens of curiosity, and the mind begins to wonder about other possibilities, perspectives, and options.

I call them *Power Questions* because they quietly ease the sense of powerlessness that accompanies a lack of options or choices. They help tap you back into a sense of your power in your world.

I frequently use a particular *Power Question*: "I wonder what other possible options or solutions are gonna show up that I haven't even thought of yet?" Notice that this question doesn't require an answer. In fact, it even relieves the pressure to find one. Instead, it creates a little sliver of possibility that other solutions are out there even though you can't yet see them.

Another one that many of my patients with health anxiety find helpful is: "I wonder what other outcomes there could be to this that I haven't even thought of yet?" Or "What if the outcome turns out to be far less scary than I'm imagining?" This can be particularly helpful for those times when you begin to develop symptoms of illness and your mind is immediately convinced you have COVID ... cancer ... a brain tumor ... or MS, etc. Before you know it, your mind has future-tripped and mapped out your demise and has you jumping into the bottomless rabbit hole of Google research.

If you can only see all the limitations in your life, feel out of options, or feel convinced there's only one possible outcome, I invite you to play with these *Power Questions*. The ones I listed above are just a handful. In truth, an endless number of *Power Questions* can be created. Notice how it feels when you pose the question to your thinking mind. Sometimes one question feels better than another, so play around a bit.

Often when you pose the question that's the right fit for that moment, you will feel something in you relax a little. You'll feel a sliver of hope move through as your thinking mind taps back into a bit of curiosity. These questions can soften the rigidity that comes when your thinking mind feels overwhelmed and out of options. And your feeling of powerlessness can ease.

It continues to amaze me how kiddos can remind us of what's true simply by being themselves. As my daughter sat under her umbrella in the rain, reading to her heart's content, she reminded me there are many ways to view our circumstances, and more options than our thinking minds might have us believe.

Remember, *Power Questions* are another great tool when your sense of possibilities feels limited, and uncertainty is present. These are questions you pose but purposefully don't answer. You simply pose the question and then ask your inner compass, wise self, nature, God, or the Universe to take care of the solutions. The questions help you shift away from having your brain work so hard to find the answers, which only feeds your stress and anxiety. Instead, they help you tap into more peace.

Try them on and see if any of them give you that "Ahhhhh, something in me just relaxed a little" feeling. Different questions will fit different circumstances.

- I wonder what other possible options or solutions will show up that I haven't even thought of yet?

- What if this ends up being easier?

- What if the outcome turns out to be far less scary than I'm imagining?

- What if it turns out there's no wrong decision here?

- What if more possibilities are coming that I haven't even thought of yet?

- I wonder what unexpected places my power will show up through this?

- What if it turns out relief is around the corner today?

- What if my stress is about to shift, and I don't know how yet?

- How can I trust even more that my wise self, higher power, intuition, God, the Universe, nature, (whatever resonates for you) has my back in this?

- I wonder what the best part of today will be?

- How can I make this easier?

- What might help me remember how many millions of things in my body are working *so* well even while I'm experiencing these other symptoms?

- What if more ease will be a part of this experience than I can imagine right now?

- What if this experience is leading me through and to incredible growth?

- What if my whole life is changing in amazing ways because of this experience?

The above are just a few examples of *Power Questions*. Feel free to create your own too. They often start with "I wonder ..." or "What if it turns out ..."

The truth is that when we're in the midst of uncertainty or facing something unknown, it can be damn uncomfortable. And it's an ordinary time for our lens of wrongness to take over. This is why our human instinct is often to double down and work relentlessly to find the answers and fixes, sometimes even forcing solutions simply to relieve the anxiety triggered by the uncertainty. I'm not suggesting we rid ourselves of our human desire to find answers, nor am I implying it's wrong for us to attempt to gain a sense of control in out-of-control circumstances!

What I am proposing are tools that can be utilized amid uncertainty to invite a shift from a lens of wrongness to curiosity. And yet again, we see this shift to curiosity usher in clarity and relief with more ease. Micro-moment pauses in the present moment offer this. *Soft I Don't Knows* can do this. *Power Questions* can provide this as well. When you're facing an overwhelming unknown, or you're grappling with the anxiety that accompanies uncertainty in some area of your life, try these tools and see which ones help you shift into curiosity. You may just discover this allows you to more easily navigate some of the hard moments along the way.

Chapter Nine

ANXIETY CAN CHANGE YOUR LIFE ... IN A GOOD WAY!

"Are you seriously going to wear *that* today? And what's up with your hair? Also, why in the *world* did you say that to Yvette yesterday? You sounded like a narcissistic jerk. Did you see her reaction? She definitely won't want to hang out any-more. Way to go." These were the kinds of words I heard in my head day in and day out. For the longest time, I tried to survive Anxiety's meanness as it hadn't occurred to me that I could try to get rid of her. But once that idea dawned, oh, baby, did I try.

Anxiety and I were roommates for a super long time. And I came to hate her. I know, I know. I'm not supposed to say I hate anyone, but I did. Over the years, she honestly became my enemy. She regularly woke me in the night to point out more ways I'd fucked up. Can you even imagine? In the middle of my sound sleep, she'd start needling me. If I tried to ignore her, she only prodded harder. She'd bring up something I'd just done and criticize me about it. Or she'd home in on inter-actions I'd had years earlier and pick me apart about how I'd handled them. She was equally skilled in pointing out how I would likely handle something terribly in the future.

Her presence overwhelmed and enraged me. I felt so pow-erless to change the one thing I was convinced was driving so many of the challenges in my life—*her*. Our contentious rela-tionship left me in a perpetual state of stress. I found it tricky to relax because I always tried to anticipate her next move and respond quickly enough to shut down Anxiety. She was just so damn judgmental and demanding. I told myself her standards were unreasonable and even ridiculous, yet they invariably climbed inside my head and gnawed at me. You know what else? My body came to have a specific response to her words. Whether it was during the day or in the middle of the night, hearing her words was always followed by a hot wave of shame that coursed through me as my focus again turned toward what was wrong with me. Having her around made it harder for me to notice anything about myself that was right, which was not exactly a boost to my self-confidence.

Once I realized I didn't *have* to live in that kind of a hostile environment, I worked like hell to find ways to get her to move out. I saw numerous therapists over these years, searching for techniques to once and for all end my dysfunctional relationship with Anxiety. I read countless self-help books on the subject. Sometimes the techniques worked for a bit, and I'd get a short-lived reprieve because she'd quiet down or seem to move out. But it was never long before she came storming back, which made me terribly disappointed in my lack of strength to stand up to Anxiety and force her to leave.

Are you ready to hear the craziest part of this whole story? We *still* live together, but she's no longer my enemy. In fact, if you can even believe it, I feel close to her now. She's not around quite as often as she once was, but when she is, my heart feels tenderness toward her. Oh, I can't even wait to tell you how this happened!

Anxiety and I have lived together for what seems like a bajillion years. I really did hate her, and I really *was* convinced the only way things would get better was if I could once and for all get rid of her. And it turns out none of that was necessary for me to find relief, which was the ultimate surprise.

The incredibly adversarial relationship I described above reflects the relationship many of us end up having with the unwanted parts of ourselves that express anxiety, perfection-ism, people-pleasing, depression, addiction, disordered eat-ing, resentment, jealousy, anger, sadness, or fear, to name a few. These parts can become so loud that we easily come to believe they define us as a whole. Yet it turns out that when we do everything in our power to fight against these unwelcome aspects of ourselves to shut them down or get rid of them, it *is* like being in a war except this war is taking place *inside* our own bodies. And this inner war impacts our nervous systems. It puts us in a perpetual stress response. It isn't simply the stress around us in our lives that's contributing to the stress we're experiencing. It's also the inner war that further compounds the stress response in our body.

Before I break down *how* my relationship with Anxiety changed drastically, I want to tell you more about some specific ways I routinely responded to Anxiety when she showed up. This is important for me to share because it was literally impos-sible for me to change my relationship with her until I recog-nized *how* I responded to her in the first place. In fact, for many years, I didn't even know to call her Anxiety! I simply knew that whenever that certain feeling showed up in me, it felt so unbear-able that I wanted it gone. Even though I'd responded to that feeling the same way for decades, I was completely oblivious to what my response was. I simply went through the motions. There's a good chance you're unaware of how you respond to your anxiety or other unwelcome parts of you. You may not even realize you have a roommate named Anxiety, as many sim-ply think of themselves as worriers or as easily stressed. Our response to Anxiety is often a default reaction we learned long ago, and it takes over as we try to manage the unbearable dis-comfort accompanying Anxiety's presence.

First, let me tell you about my fear of public speaking because it was in this arena that my relationship with Anxiety first began to transform. In truth, this fear was bigger than public speaking. It was anything that required me to give an answer, state an opinion, or perform in front of others as these situations all increased the risk that my inner, innate wrongness would be exposed. It showed up in class, where I rarely raised my hand voluntarily unless I was extremely confident in a particular course. If I was spontaneously called on, I immediately felt like I was drowning; my mind would go completely blank, my face would turn deep red, and the shaking would begin. My mind and body felt convinced I was going to die. Of course, I was skilled at hiding my shakes because I'd had so many years honing that skill in church! But it was hard to hide the red face or my lack of an answer due to my blank mind. Hot shame would wash over me on repeat for weeks, months, and even years to come whenever I thought back to that moment when I was called on and did not have a self-assured answer. You can see why I avoided being called on at all costs. The feeling it produced in me was so unbearable that I routinely tried to be invisible, sitting in the back row, trying not to stand out.

Whenever a class required that each student memorize a poem and stand up in front of the class to recite it, I always tried to be the last person to do so. I was convinced that postponing it made it more tolerable than getting it out of the way. Instead, I believe it just made the pain last longer, but it seemed worth it in those moments. Anxiety even showed up in medical school when we had to perform physical exams in front of supervisors so they could evaluate our skills. The anticipatory anxiety I experienced leading up to these evaluations was almost intolerable. No matter how long and hard I studied and no matter how well I knew the material, when it was my turn to perform the exam, my mind would momentarily go blank, triggering a full-on panic attack inside my body. Again, it's unlikely that many could tell how big my panic was because I was skilled at keeping it on the inside while covering up most of it on the outside. This panic even showed up in Al-Anon meetings I attended. Whenever I shared in the group, my hands and legs trembled, and my heart raced. Interestingly, my panic always turned down a notch if I made anyone laugh while I shared. Looking back, I can appreciate how this was reassuring to the part of me that was so worried I wasn't going to share in the "right" way.

When I look back on those endless times when Anxiety showed up, I can see how instantly my default response occurred. The second that Anxiety landed in my body, I tightened, attempting to thwart an all-out takeover. My default response was to fight and try like hell to get rid of her. I couldn't see any other way to find relief. Do you recall my example of the hand and fist in chapter three: *How to Experience the Power of the Micro-Moment ... Right Now?* That's what I was doing in my default response, trying to pry Anxiety out of my fist, but this only resulted in the fist resisting and tightening more, further pinning Anxiety in place. Did this response keep me in the present moment? Not one bit. In fact, it required that I check out of the present moment altogether because it was so unbearable. No wonder my mind so frequently went blank because I wasn't even home inside myself. As Anxiety spiraled, my inner dialogue always ramped up. "What the fuck is wrong with you? Get your shit together, Emily. Why are you making this evaluation such a big deal? Look at everyone else; *they're* not freaking out like this. Focus already. Oh, great, now you're gonna get it wrong and everyone's gonna see." I only knew how to look around at others and notice how they seemed to be performing and compare myself to their experience, which was a surefire way to worsen my anxiety.

But in my forties, a new perspective came along that changed the game for me. I began to understand that Anxiety was just *one* part of me, not all of me. I wasn't initially convinced of this, but as I played with this concept, I started to feel a difference. What did this practice look like? Well, in one instance, I was a bridesmaid in a friend's wedding. She asked if I would be willing to give a toast at her reception. Of course, I said yes because I didn't want to let her down, but I was terrified! I even put off writing the toast until the last minute to avoid feeling my anxiety around it.

In the thirty minutes leading up to my toast, my anxiety became almost intolerable with the shakes taking over, my heart pounding, dizziness settling in and my mind having trouble thinking straight. I sneaked to a private room away from the reception area, sat down, and practiced the *Micro-Moment Reset* I discussed in chapter three. I noticed sensations of tightness and panic were especially strong in my chest, so I sat and talked to Anxiety. I said, "Oh, yeah, I can feel how scared you're feeling right now. I'm right here with you. Whatever you're feeling right now is totally OK. I just wanna be here with you while you're feeling it." I didn't try to stop Anxiety or get rid of her. I didn't make her wrong for being there. I didn't tell her all the reasons she didn't need to be anxious. I simply allowed her to be anxious and kept her company. And the strangest thing began to happen. I felt something in my soul relax. It was as if Anxiety gave a little sigh of relief even though my physical symptoms didn't change. And then it was time, and I went out there, gave my toast, and survived it!

There was something about that sigh of relief I felt in my soul that I couldn't get past. I wanted more of it. I started practicing the *Micro-Moment Reset* more regularly when Anxiety showed up. I didn't always remember to do this. That deeply ingrained default response to fight against Anxiety showed up regularly. Still, a few minutes into that response I sometimes remembered to pause and turn *toward* Anxiety and be present with her for a few moments. Each time I did this, I felt that inner sigh of relief deep in my soul. My spinning mind slowed down. I felt more grounded and less panicky. My physical symptoms began to turn down more as I continued to play with this tool too. *This was honestly shocking.* It almost seemed like a trick. I'd spent forty-some-odd years believing the only way to survive Anxiety was to wage a war against her. Yet I found the relief when I turned toward Anxiety, permitted her to feel whatever she was feeling, and kept her company.

This was the first approach I'd ever tried that resulted in lasting and repeatable relief. I was finding it so helpful for myself that I began to wonder if it might be helpful for my oldest daughter. She has her own roommate named Anxiety, likely inherited from yours truly. For years, whenever Anxiety showed up for her, I spent hours at a time sitting with her and lovingly telling her all the reasons she didn't need to feel anxious about whatever issue was at hand. And her Anxiety stayed and stayed and stayed. But as I practiced this new tool myself, I realized what I was *actually* telling her when I pointed out all the reasons she didn't need to feel anxious. *I was telling her that her anxiety was wrong.* But here's the tricky part: whether it was wrong or not, it was there. My words unknowingly showed her that Anxiety was her enemy too. This was horrifying to realize. And as mothers so easily do, I promptly worried I'd permanently scarred her with my response to her Anxiety.

I decided to try my new approach with her to see if it might help. She showed up with big anxiety soon after that. I sat down on the couch with her and said, "Oh, honey, yeah. I can feel how anxious and worried you're feeling. I'm gonna sit here with you while you're feeling this. We can snuggle if you want. But I just want to be here with you while you're feeling this." She snuggled in. And I'm not even kidding. Within *two minutes* she'd moved through her anxiety and was off and running to play with her sister. It took me at least ten minutes to scrape my chin off the floor. I thought, "What the hell just happened?" because these episodes of anxiety usually lasted *hours.* Do you notice how possible it was for her to respond differently to her anxiety when neither of us was fighting against it but instead was simply acknowledging its presence and creating space for it to be there too? Just like the hand and fist example in chapter three, we shifted from trying to pry the anxiety out of that fist to simply holding the fist while the anxiety was in it. This small shift made an entirely new response possible.

Does this mean this approach is the holy grail to solving all anxiety? Nah, of course not. But it gives us a starting point for creating new neural pathways. These make new responses to anxiety possible, which was once impossible to even imagine. Over time, my relationship with this part of me named Anxiety has grown and deepened. In truth, my relationship with *many* parts of me has grown.

A NEW RELATIONSHIP WITH ANXIETY

I started playing with the *Who's Knocking?* tool I mentioned in chapter three. When Anxiety descended, I'd spend a few micro-moments getting quiet and going inside myself. I imagined I was home alone and heard a knock at the door. When I opened the door, Anxiety was the one who had knocked and was waiting outside the door. I got to see who Anxiety was. In this practice, I often see an actual person or a child on the other side of that door. Others who practice this will see a person, shape, image, or color. Or they simply sense or hear the presence without seeing anything. For me, my Anxiety part is always a young girl. What I've learned is that none of these parts that live in us have any interest in us "fixing" how they're feeling. They simply want to be seen and acknowledged by us. They ache for permission to feel whatever they're feeling. It's our acknowledgment and presence with them that brings relief, not us fixing them. This is distinctly counter to how our minds learn to think about unwanted feelings.

It's easy to feel convinced that we need to get in there and fix these feelings so they go away. But in truth, most of us have spent a lifetime trying to push away the parts of us that show up bearing unwelcome feelings. This means these parts of us have been navigating these big, uncomfortable feelings on their own inside us all this time. This is why it's so powerful when we pause to be present with them, the same way I was with my daughter when I tried it differently that day. Our presence and acknowledgment of what these parts are feeling enable them to update their beliefs over time as they experience us continuing to be there for them. These parts of us begin to learn that there's room for their feelings, no matter how uncomfortable. Their intolerable feelings become more tolerable. And I can't begin to emphasize how powerful this tool becomes with practice.

For many, learning to navigate big, hard feelings all on your own as a child can leave you convinced you can't count on support from others. It can even leave parts of you believing you aren't good enough, you don't count as others do, or there's something innately wrong with you. This is why taking micro-moments to show up for these parts inside us is so damn transformative. The parts begin to have a different experience that repeatedly reflects to them that they matter to us or we wouldn't be showing up to be with them while they're feeling unbearable feelings like anxiety. It ultimately enables these parts of us to update their beliefs and perspectives. And this changes how easily they're triggered and how they can move through the world in which we live.

As you read this, it's possible you're thinking, "Yup, this book was working for me till now. But all this talk about parts living inside me and the suggestion that I talk with these different parts ... ummm, it's sounding pretty damn woo woo!" And I agree. It *does* sound different. I wasn't sure about it at first either until I started playing with the idea and found, for the first time in my life, that I experienced internal relief whenever I connected with a part of myself. It was a relief I'd hunted and ached for for so long. I'd virtually given up hope that relief was even possible for me. And then it was.

Anxiety and I still live together. But my response to her has changed when she shows up. It used to be, "God dammit, noooo! I don't want you here. What's it gonna take to get rid of you?" But now, it's more commonly, "Oh, hey. It's you again." I feel tenderness as I say this. I wouldn't believe it myself if I hadn't experienced it thousands of times. When Anxiety is triggered in me, I more often remember to turn toward her with curiosity instead of viewing her through a lens of wrongness and waging a war. I spend micro-moments of time acknowledging how she's feeling, being present with her, and making space for her anxiety to just be. This creates a different response in my nervous system. It naturally shifts from the sympathetic, fight-or-flight response to the calmer, parasympathetic response. Do I always remember to turn toward my anxiety? Nope. As humans, none of us will *ever* master any of this perfectly. But that's the magical thing about this approach! We *never* have to do it perfectly for it to work.

If the concepts in this chapter leave you skeptically curious, good. I wouldn't expect it to all make sense just yet. The truth is that anxiety has many faces, including perfectionism, people-pleasing, fear of judgment, and uncertainty. The good news is that these faces of anxiety lose their grip when we shift from a lens of wrongness to one of curiosity.

Chapter Ten

ARE YOU A PERFECTIONIST? IF SO, I'LL BET YOU HAVE AN INNER BULLY!

In March of sixth grade, I transferred to a new school. But here's the catch: I went back into the fifth grade because there was no room left in the sixth grade that late in the year. Oy. I hated having to repeat part of fifth grade. I hated being so tall compared to the other kids. I hated that I was the only one wearing a bra.

I hated the bullies in my new class even more. It started with small things like stealing my fancy pencils and little notepads and throwing them into the toilet. After a week or so, these girls began climbing over the toilet stall to taunt me. Or they circled me during recess and asked why I was twelve when everyone else was ten or eleven. They laughed and suggested it meant I was stupid. The ringleader repeatedly informed me that her mom thought I was a dog.

I'd never before been bullied. While I didn't understand this back then, being liked by others had long been my barometer for how I was doing in the world. If people seemed pleased with me, I knew I was doing well. If they didn't, this set off alarm bells. And my inner alarm bells went wild during this time. I kicked into navigating my day from the outside in, trying to figure out others' expectations, so I would know the right way to be. I assumed this would ease the bullying, but it didn't, and the bullying quickly impacted every aspect of my life. My posture became stooped as I tried to fade into the background. I became shy and quiet, two things I'm not generally accused of. My confidence plummeted, and my sense of self took a huge hit.

To top it all off, my inner bully grew louder during this time. You know that inner voice that shows up and has a regular torrent of critical or mean things to say to you. We've *all* got this part, and it really *can* be an inner bully. It shows up saying things like, "What's wrong with you? You totally messed that up. Why the hell did you do that? What, are you an idiot? Would you just get your shit together? Ugh. God, look at you. You're so fat ... skinny ... ugly ... stupid. Why can't you look more like that girl? You're such a shitty mom. You're too much for people. You're too sensitive." And when you hear that voice inside, it can feel the same as facing an outside bully in your life. The only difference is that this inner bully goes everywhere with you. Oy.

This is important to understand. Unlike outer bullies, the inner bully is just one part of each of us. But it still feels *awful* when that inner bully part gets going. And what do you likely do when it shows up? You try to push those thoughts away or get rid of them, all while a growing worry builds in the background, telling you that the words might be accurate. In truth, it often feels like you're in a war with this inner voice and then with yourself too.

As I moved on to middle school, my inner bully grew. It became quite common for me to wash, condition, and blow-dry my hair up to *three* times before leaving for the school bus in the mornings. If I finished blow-drying my hair the first time and there were even a few strands on my head that weren't cooperating with the other hairs, I felt driven to start the whole process over again from start to finish. I wanted to be sure to get *all* the hairs just right. I'm not talking about a casual desire to fix hairs so they looked mildly decent. I'm talking about a feeling that repeatedly took over, convincing me I couldn't possibly survive and face the outside world if I didn't fix my hair perfectly first.

It was a fairly regular occurrence for me to angrily chuck my hairbrush across the bathroom as I tried not to explode with the frustration of having to start the entire wash, condition, and blow-dry sequence over again. It drove my middle sister crazy because, well, she not only had to duck when the hairbrush flew, but my lengthy hair sequence regularly made my morning routine last a lot longer, so we had to race to the bus late. I think my parents simply thought it was a tween/teen thing. I didn't think anything of it myself except that I knew no one else understood how serious it really was when my hair didn't do exactly what I believed it needed to do. I didn't understand it was my inner bully telling me my hair wasn't perfect enough or demanding I redo it. I simply thought it was me telling myself this, and I believed perfection was the only way to find relief.

MY OLDER PERFECTIONIST

As I grew older, I improved at covering how worried my appearance made me, but my drive for perfection persisted. "Clothes crises" were common, even for a casual outing. Sure, I joked with friends about it, and we laughed about these clothes crises of mine like it was a lighthearted quirkiness. But what did this look like? It involved starting with one outfit before rejecting it and pulling other options out of my closet and drawers until half of my wardrobe was strewn all over my bed and floor while I panicked in search of the "right" outfit. Again, the underlying feeling was that I would not be able to survive and face the world if I didn't find the perfect outfit. Talk about exhausting. I secretly ached to be one of those girls who casually tossed clothes on, brushed her hair, and ran out the door.

Interestingly, it was when I began dating a woman for the first time that my anxiety about my appearance unexpectedly began to soften. It felt surprising … amazing … and confusing. I've had many years to watch this shift continue since then and I've come to feel such tenderness and love for my younger self as my understanding of her anxieties has deepened. We all have our outside selves we share with the world. It was the part of me that I tried to make look perfect. But what about how we feel on the inside? What happens when we learn to believe that our inside self is wrong, unlovable, broken, can't be trusted, or needs to be disregarded altogether? Or that our outside self cannot rely on our inside self for guidance?

It puts that much more pressure on your outside self to keep things looking good, even perfect, in the hope of decreasing the chance that someone might detect the wrongness, unlovableness, or not-good-enoughness that you're convinced makes up the core of who you are. It doesn't help that we see perfection as the standard against which we measure ourselves in our culture. We learn to believe that certain emotions or experiences are considered acceptable, and others aren't. Some choices or looks are deemed right and others wrong. We're constantly fed messages in the media and culture that our imperfect, human selves need to be fixed, enhanced, or corrected, and we try to meet these unrealistic expectations. Notice the lens of wrongness at play here too.

I can look back now and see how my inside self was convinced I was wrong or bad. And the truth is, so many walk around with this same belief tucked inside them. If you're someone who feels convinced that something is innately wrong with you or that you are broken, worthless, or unlovable, you're not alone. If your inner bully repeatedly tries to convince you that perfection is the only acceptable standard to try and offset these inner feelings, you're also not alone. Twenty years ago, I wouldn't have believed my own inside beliefs would or even could shift and soften. It felt like a cross

I simply had to bear. And yet my experience with my inner bully *has* changed, as has my relationship with perfection.

Many patients ask me what they need to do to eliminate their inner bully. And oh, do I get it. I battled mine for a long time. But here's what I've learned. Fighting against your inner bully doesn't get rid of it. In truth, if anything, this ultimately makes it louder. But becoming curious about what's driving your inner bully beneath all the mean words and judgment? Now that's revolutionary.

For eons, my inner bully spent endless energy telling me my outfits or hair weren't perfect. Or that my house wasn't flawlessly cleaned and organized before guests came over. Or that I hadn't interacted in just the right way when I socialized with someone. When I took these words seriously, they left me feeling *terrible*. And desperate to be different from how I was in my appearance, behaviors, or person. You may relate in some way.

Here's the wild thing I've come to know and trust, though: something unexpected happens when we pause the fight against our inner bully, pause the automatic assumption that it's wrong, and turn toward it with even the tiniest inkling of curiosity. Yes, curiosity changed this experience for me. It invited me to look beneath the words and wonder *why* this part of me wanted my hair or outfits to be perfect in the first place. *Why* was this part so afraid to have my house "lived-in" instead of perfect for guests? Why was it always on the lookout for the miniscule ways I hadn't handled myself perfectly in a social setting? This curiosity repeatedly led me back to the same discovery. My inner bully believed if I didn't look or behave a certain way, others would discover the truth about my inside self, no longer like me, or reject me altogether and go away. It believed perfection made me worthy of others' love and presence.

Realizing this offered me a surprisingly fresh perspective.

I understood *why* my inner bully worked so hard to point out and critique my "imperfections." A strange appreciation crept in for the commitment this bully displayed as it repeatedly attempted to "protect" me in the only way it knew how. It was trying to prevent me from being found out, rejected, and abandoned by others.

You CAN Enjoy Life Before It's Perfect

There's another way our inner bully's expectations of perfection sneak into our lives: when it tries to convince us that we must make certain aspects of our lives perfect before we can really start living and enjoying life. This means that our anxiety ... chronic illness ... cancer ... fatigue ... miserable job ... unhappy marriage ... physical appearance ... or hopelessness about the state of our country or world hinder our ability to embrace the moment we're in and find joy.

For a long time, I believed this. That if I worked hard enough to get things *just right*, then I could *really* start living and enjoying my life. But this requires that we constantly hunt for what's wrong in our lives so we can make the wrongs right. It makes perfection a prerequisite to enjoying life. Uh oh. That sounds challenging and exhausting.

There's a catch to living in the wrongness of our lives all the time. Have you ever noticed that when you focus on what's wrong or imperfect, it automatically pulls you out of the present and into the past or future? We're either reminiscing about how our lives were once better, or focused on a particular goal in our future that will hold relief. But where does that leave the present moment we're experiencing? Does it make it go away? Does a focus on the past or the future make our current feelings any less present? Definitely not.

What I've learned is that there are often gems cloaked within the apparent wrongness of the present moment. Sometimes the seeming wrongness is truly beckoning us back into the present, where it's more possible to create a different relationship with the very thing we thought we needed to overcome.

My post-thyroidectomy adventure reminded me of this as I worked to find the right balance of thyroid medication that my body is now dependent on. I didn't plan to have such a tricky time with this. In fact, I envisioned the opposite, so you can imagine how wrong it felt when it was so difficult for me to balance my new medication. My mind thought about how much better it had been when my thyroid was present and could balance things for me. I focused on how incorrect the current dose felt and how badly I wanted to reach a specific time when my dose would finally and forever be balanced. I was grounded in the past and the future. Yet there was no room for me to be present and live in the now if I was always waiting for that elusive, future day that would finally make the present right for me.

One day, I was walking the dog and quietly stewing about my frustration with this whole thyroid-dosing escapade. I found myself saying, "Emily, you know what? Maybe you're never going to find the perfect dose. Maybe this thyroid medication dance will be a part of your experience for the rest of your life." Shockingly, my present moment immediately felt less wrong. Even my feelings of frustration felt less wrong. Why is this? Because these questions created space for the present moment to be here. They cracked the door for a new relationship to form with the very experience I'd been so busy trying to get out of. As surprising as it may sound, I felt relieved to realize that I might never reach a perfect thyroid medication dose. It unexpectedly took the pressure off me to have to work so hard to try and reach that elusive perfect dose. There was room for this thyroid medication dance *and* for me to be engaged with my life and its various joys.

UGLY GAVE ME GIFTS

I had a similar experience when menopause hit in my late forties, which happened to coincide with my thyroid cancer. My body, skin, and hair were changing in new ways, and I didn't like it. Not one bit. I felt ugly. Really ugly. All I could think about was the physical appearance I used to have, and what I needed to do to "fix" myself so I could get back to my pre-menopausal, pre-thyroid cancer state that had become my vision of perfection. Of course, social media didn't help my plight. Each time I sat down to peruse others' posts, ads popped up showing me exactly how to fix my skin, lose weight, or grow luscious locks again. The more ads like this I clicked, the more ads Facebook and Instagram's algorithms sent promising the holy grail of solutions for my physical changes. I not only kept clicking on those damn ads, but I also fell for many of them, ordering creams or signing up for various advertised exercise programs! Did these products help shift me back into my vision of perfection? No, dammit.

I hated how I felt during this time. My lens of wrongness convinced me I needed to figure out how to stop feeling ugly so I could finally feel better and start living again. My mind believed the way to do this was to find ways to fix my hair, skin, and body so they looked like they did before. It argued that my prior physical appearance was perfect compared to now, which is a regular riot considering none of it felt perfect to me back then.

After *many* months of swimming through the uglies, I went to the mall. As I passed various store windows, I saw outfits on skinny mannequins, and my repeated thought was, "Gosh, I love that outfit! That's so my style. I wanna try it on." These thoughts were immediately followed by a response from my inner bully, who declared, "Who are you kidding? You haven't been able to wear an outfit like that in fifteen years. Face it, those days are over, darlin'." It's hard enough to feel insecure, let alone ugly, but to have our inner bullies compound this by hurling critical words at us is painful. And it's also a reality for so many of us.

My mind swam with all the possible ways I might be able to fix my appearance so I could feel more acceptable in the world. But an unexpected thought shot through my mind. I wasn't at war with my skin, body, or hair. I was in a war with my *feeling* of ugliness. I was looking for anything that would stop me from *feeling* ugly. And this was a big relief for me to realize. I'd already learned that it simply doesn't work to fight against a feeling we're experiencing. (Remember the hand and fist example in chapter three?) When we fight against an emotion, it only grows louder in us because our feelings yearn for our acknowledgment and presence, rather than fixing. This is what makes relief more possible. But when we fight against a feeling such as ugly, that feeling only gets louder as it tries to get our attention.

I paused in the middle of that mall, stepped back into the present moment, and acknowledged my feelings of ugliness. I whispered, "Emily, you're feeling ugly right now. This is what it feels like to have the feeling of ugliness here." I noticed the weight that sat on my shoulders while I felt ugly. I realized I was holding my shoulders up by my ears and walking with a stooped back, trying not to be seen in my ugliness.

And you know what happened? I felt a bit lighter as I finished my jaunt at the mall. I didn't feel less ugly, but I understood my relentless search for the fixes was not the thing that would usher in perfection and make this feeling go away. Instead, the part of me feeling ugly needed my acknowledgment and presence, which is what I began to give it. As I moved through the next few days, pausing to acknowledge the presence of this part of me that felt so ugly, something strange happened. I began to feel less ugly. I kid you not. Absolutely nothing about my body had changed, yet I felt different about it on the inside.

It's incredibly empowering to discover that joy, peace, and relief are possible even *while* we're going through challenging experiences or emotions. It makes room for new relationships to form with the very parts of ourselves that have felt so wrong. Our lens of wrongness convinces us these parts of us need to be perfected, fixed, fought against, or downright resolved before we can really get to living our best lives. Yet we continue to see that curiosity becomes the soothing antidote when it's included in these unwanted experiences or emotions. Surprisingly, relief becomes more possible in the midst of it all.

Intrigued? I hope so because it's equally possible for you to update your relationship and experience with both perfection and *your* inner bully. If you're ready to do this, play with the following steps and see what you find:

- **Invite yourself to notice when your inner bully is present.** Often, it's been spewing mean words, judgments, and expectations of perfection in the background for so long that it's easy to become numb to its presence. Yet its words continue to take a toll. In the beginning, there will be *many* times when you fail to recognize its presence, so celebrate the times when you *do* notice it.

- **Welcome curiosity to the scene.** Notice the words your inner bully is spewing. Then look beneath the words and invite yourself to look beyond the face value of your inner bully's words. Become curious about what might be driving those words in the first place. Wonder what feeling(s) it might be trying to protect you from with its words, judgments, or expectations? For example, if it's telling you that you can't possibly accomplish a dream you have because you're not smart enough, it may believe these words will prevent you from taking a risk that could lead to failure. Perhaps this part of you believes failure will lead others to discover how wrong and unworthy you really are. Remember, the inner bully's goal is to protect us from experiencing even more unbearable feelings than what it's spewing.

- **Appreciate your inner bully's commitment to protecting you, even if you *hate* the *way* it's doing it.** Give yourself time to become comfortable with this step. There's a reason I didn't list this as the first step! It's stunning how responsive the inner bully is to being acknowledged for how hard it's been working and appreciated for its commitment. Believe it or not, these inner bullies are often exhausted and would love a different role, but never before knew this was a possibility. What can this sound like? "Oh, hey. I want you to know I hear you. I recognize that you're working hard to try to protect me right now. I appreciate how committed you are." It is *not* necessary to offer appreciation for *how* it is trying to protect you!

As you gently play with these three steps over time, there's a good chance you will notice an updated relationship forming between you, your inner bully, your anxiety and your accompanying perfectionism. You might even become less quick to take your bully's words at face value. It'll become easier to take micro-moment pauses to wonder what's *driving* your bully's demand for perfection. And shockingly, you may even find yourself appreciating how committed your bully has been to trying to "protect" you all this time. *That* is where the magic happens, and your inner bully begins to soften as it feels your appreciation for its intentions. Your inside and outside selves begin to work as a team. Now isn't that worth exploring?

Chapter Eleven

THE SURPRISING ANTIDOTE TO PEOPLE-PLEASING

In first grade, I frequently sidled up to my teacher and quietly informed her that one classmate or another was crying. I did this the whole year. And it repeatedly surprised my teacher because she hadn't noticed anyone crying. To this day, I can smell a cry from a mile away! No joke. I always notice people crying or feeling upset or anxious long before the rest of the crowd does. This is a gift. It's certainly served me as a naturopathic doctor and therapist. But gifts are funny sometimes. We can put them to use in ways that serve us and others. Or we can apply them in ways that begin to move us out of balance.

As I navigated life while being sensitive, I became quite sponge-like. Perhaps you know what I'm talking about. I'd easily absorb the discomfort, pain, anxiety, or sadness that anyone around me was experiencing. In fact, I often went so far as to almost feel their pain *for* them. Growing up in a family impacted by alcoholism, it's not surprising that my focus went to the well-being of others. It's a smart, creative way to try to keep the others around you happy in an attempt to feel more in control and keep things more predictable. The reality is that many different experiences can cause you to place your focus wholeheartedly on others, which leads to this creative way of trying to cope. These experiences often foster a sensitivity in you that can go on to be such a gift in your life, unless that gift swings too far out of balance. That's when others' needs become way more important than your own. In fact, you often stop counting altogether.

One way my gift of sensitivity moved out of balance over time was with my people-pleasing tendencies. Oh, boy, did I learn how to throw myself into trying to please everyone around me. My first-grade ability to read the room only grew as I did. I instinctually scanned whatever room or environment I was in, assessing how others felt. When I detected an upset feeling or need in someone, I felt the compulsion to address it, and I don't use the word compulsion lightly. I was convinced it was *my* sole responsibility to help that person. At home, this meant the second I sensed anger in my parents, I threw myself and my sisters into cleaning and organizing the house. My sisters still joke about how I bossed them into cleaning mode with me! Outside the home, I was uber-responsible, readily helping friends' parents unload their groceries, prepare dinner at a sleepover, or help in any other useful way. I often stepped in to offer help before the other person even identified a need for it.

Over the years, my need to please showed up in new ways as I honed my ability to help others with their emotions. Whether it was a stranger or a person I knew, many turned to me for help when they were navigating hard feelings or experiences. I became excellent at responding to crises too. It turns out I'm a good one to have around for those! Some freeze in the face of a crisis, but my body responds and tackles a crisis before I realize I'm responding. I often jump out of the car at the site of a motor vehicle accident and rush to give aid. I'm regularly shocked to find myself running to the crash because my body responds before my brain does. This happened long before I ever became a doctor, and back then, I often wondered what I thought I was going to do to help when I had no medical training, yet my body thought otherwise.

People-pleasing is tricky. It has two sides. It can certainly lead to accolades. You throw yourself into people-pleasing, constantly reading the room, and detecting the needs of those around you. You repeatedly attempt to meet those needs, which often leads to accolades because you're helping so much, working so hard, or accomplishing and persevering under challenging circumstances. These accolades make us feel good, boost our sense of worth, make us feel needed, and sometimes even give us a temporary high. But there's another side to people-pleasing that's more subtle. The lens of wrongness so easily slips in and quietly invites us to navigate life from the outside in again. Our focus shifts outside ourselves as we determine what our next move is according to the needs of others. This can easily drive us to disregard the nudges and needs of our inside self and view them as wrong.

You might not even notice that your own needs are not counting. But over time, as the people-pleasing persists, it begins to feel like others aren't making you count or that you don't matter to them. I know this feeling well and you may too. That old familiar feeling creeps back in, just under the surface, and you again doubt your worth. You're increasingly convinced that you must prove you are good and worthy of others' love. It becomes impossible to believe that worth and goodness have been inherently yours since before you took your first breath. Instead, you're certain you must continue to earn it.

And this becomes damn tiring, always striving to prove yourself. The lens of wrongness slips in, persuading you that you are intrinsically wrong and must earn your rightness. At some point in the relentless people-pleasing game, resentment kicks in. You start feeling pissed that you're giving so much to these folks around you and that they're taking advantage of your kindness. You might even feel terribly unappreciated. This little factor often goes unseen but drives this whole experience. It allows your gift of sensitivity and caring to stop feeling like a gift. When *you* don't matter to you, your gift of caring for others can no longer be used in a balanced way. It's impossible. Sure, you may be able to pull it off for a stint, but the positive feelings you gain from helping others can't last when you don't treat yourself like you matter to you.

It starts with the little ways we disregard ourselves. You offer to help a friend even though you're running on fumes that day. You skip eating because there's no time for it when you have so much to take care of. You agree to meet up with a colleague who's having a hard time even though you don't want to go for any number of reasons. You let go of your self-care routine because there's simply no time for it with others' needs. Yet there's a more monumental way we disregard ourselves that packs the most punch: *when we pay so much attention to others' feelings and needs, we can no longer connect with our own.* This ends up driving *all* the other, bigger choices we make when we disregard ourselves. When the balance is off-kilter, it's easy to become so busy taking care of everyone else around you with your gifts and big heart that you don't even realize what *you* are feeling and needing on the inside. You lose touch with your inner compass and your inside self.

I Smiled the Wrong Way

I was fourteen when I walked into the locker room and smiled at my basketball coach as she passed me. She didn't smile back. That's all it took for me to panic that I hadn't smiled the right way, or she would have returned my smile. I immediately went to the mirror in the bathroom and re-created the smile I'd given to analyze how I could have done it differently.

This is such a vivid memory for me. And I have thousands more that reflect this same fear, each with a different scenario, but the underlying anxiety remained: if I didn't please people, they would think badly of me and wouldn't like me. Having others like me and feeling connected to those around me was my barometer for how I was doing in the world. Whenever I came across someone who didn't seem to like me, I literally felt like I might die.

This desire to please others started early. I remember being around five years old when I painstakingly washed and then powdered the upstairs bathroom door. I spent a good while focused on this seemingly important cleaning endeavor. I *must* have been young because who powders a door anyway? The whole while, I kept thinking, "Maybe now Mommy will think I'm as good as she was when she was a kid!" We loved to listen to my mom tell stories about her childhood, and she had many. But I was also eager to hear stories of times she'd misbehaved, and she only had a couple of those stories to share, and they were times she'd unintentionally misbehaved. When asked about this, she explained that she'd been a notably good kid. And in my five-year-old mind, I took this to mean I had some work to do because I knew I regularly did things that got me in trouble!

This belief that I was a bad kid and my desire to be good and please others only continued. I suspect the secrecy around my sexual abuse compounded this as it convinced me I had to keep my "badness" a secret or others would treat me differently. Being mannerly, well-behaved, and responsible felt immensely important to me. It's probably why I became such a rule follower. Oh, boy. Breaking the rules, any rules, was almost unbearable to me. Even today, there are times when I have to pep-talk myself into breaking a rule, even when it's a stupid one! As I mentioned, I often experienced this need to be good in church. My mom regularly returned from church to mention that one parishioner or another had commented on how well-behaved and mannerly we were that day. I could feel this made my mom proud, so I felt proud too. I didn't understand back then that underneath my pride was an already solid belief that pleasing those around me helped me hide my badness.

I took a unique class in my last year of college that required each student write to individuals who knew us as young kids and ask them to describe us back then. The contents of the letters I received from aunts, grandmothers, and old babysitters took me by surprise. They *all* talked about what a sweet, sensitive, thoughtful, and well-behaved kid I was. That was the first moment I realized my own memories of myself as a kid drastically differed. I only remembered being too much, frequently going too far, being annoying, getting in trouble, and being "naughty." Isn't that wild? This information compelled me to ask my parents about *their* memories of me as a young kid, and I was sure their answers would validate my own. But shock of all shocks, their descriptions of me lined up with those in the letters I'd received. At the time, this was so confusing to me.

This belief that I was a bad kid on the inside had been part of my life for so long that I didn't even realize it was a belief. It was simply a fact that lived inside me. I didn't understand that an immense fear drove my desire to please everyone around me. I had no idea. I just knew I felt *terrible* when I didn't please anyone or – God forbid – disappointed someone. The unbearable feelings triggered so much anxiety that I did almost anything to avoid them. It turns out a common way to try to distract yourself from unbearable feelings is to simply *think* incessantly about the details of the situation that triggered them. You review what happened, who said or did what, who was right, and who was wrong. You create stories about what the other person was thinking or feeling. And then you replay imaginary do-over or follow-up conversations with that person. Of course, these imaginary conversations are often tense and involve speaking your mind and proving to the other person that you are right. Oh, and let's not forget how often all this thinking takes place in the middle of the night when you are trying to sleep!

Does this thinking make the dread and anxiety go away?

Not one bit. It continues to sit there like dead weight just under the surface of all the thinking. The thinking is simply an attempt to distract you from it. People-pleasing is exhausting. But so is feeling like you aren't good enough or are a bad person deep down. It leaves you with an endless need to prove yourself. People liking you becomes the barometer for how you're doing in the world. It also prevents you from hearing the call of your inner compass as it continuously tries to remind you of what it truly knows: you are worthy, you are gifted, you are loved, you are wise, and peace is woven into your very essence. Who you are here to be in the world is *so* beautifully enough.

THE ANTIDOTE TO PEOPLE-PLEASING: CONNECTION WITH SELF

There are so many experiences in life that can lead you to doubt your worth, convince you that you aren't enough, and fill you with anxiety. Many who feel this way grew up around addiction or dysfunction, or experienced sexual or physical abuse. Others never had these experiences, yet they still struggle with this. Let's face it, we are constantly barraged by messages in the media and culture that suggest how we feel, look, or act is not right enough and that the solutions to these "problems" lie outside us. Regardless of how you land in this place, your reaction is often the same. You try to determine your worth by pleasing and seeking approval from others. And to do this, it becomes necessary to nourish your connection with others, but not yourself.

The great news is that purposely learning to nourish our connection with ourselves is the antidote. I mean it. Sure, it doesn't happen overnight. Growing a connection with ourselves takes time, just like growing a friendship with anyone new.

But the beautiful thing is that we are fostering a new neural pathway each time we pause for a few micro-moments to come back home inside ourselves and notice what we're feeling and needing. Over time, this pathway grows stronger and allows us to have a different experience.

When I first began to play with this newer approach to my people-pleasing, it didn't change my behavior on the outside at all. To the onlooker, I continued to people-please my brains out. But on the inside, micro-moment pauses were happening. As I ran around tending to the needs of so many others around me, I took these one-to-three-second pauses to notice what I was feeling on the inside *while* I ran around. I felt different ways in these various pauses: exhausted, overstretched, overwhelmed, resentful, dizzy, hungry, thirsty, needing to use the loo. Interestingly, I normally didn't have time for these feelings when I was in my full-on people-pleasing escapades. But with these micro-moment pauses, I could notice these inner experiences for a few seconds at a time.

At first, I couldn't do more than acknowledge those inner feelings or needs in those seconds. I wasn't yet able to tend to them in any way. But do you know what happened as I continued to take those pauses and notice the experience inside myself? Those inside experiences started to matter to me a bit more. At first, it only felt possible for them to matter for two minutes, and I would quickly run to the loo, scarf down food, or guzzle gulps of water. But over time, those two minutes grew to five, which grew to ten, and I was able to tend to my needs during those minutes. Notice that I didn't feel able to express my feelings or needs to anyone outside. But acknowledging my needs to myself on the inside was a *big* change and was quietly building a new neural pathway in my brain that fostered a reconnection with myself.

Note how surreptitiously the lens of wrongness slips in to guide our experience of people-pleasing. It ushers in the all-or-nothing thinking that accompanies this lens, so we're persuaded we must people-please at any cost to ourselves. It convinces us that others' needs count while ours don't and tells us our needs are wrong for being there in the first place. It demands that we navigate life from the outside, in this case, paying more attention to the needs of others than to our own. Yet it turns out, on the inside, a quiet voice continues to whisper that we *do* matter and that our needs *must* count too. And when we create micro-moment pauses to notice what's happening for us on the inside *while* we're people-pleasing, we begin to reconnect with that quiet inner voice of guidance so we can hear it.

Have I now mastered people-pleasing, so it never happens anymore? Nah. It still shows up sometimes. But my response to it is different now. My connection with my inside self has grown. As my connection has grown, I've learned that our inner compass is always calling us back home, offering a refuge of steady peace and guidance. This means that my tolerance for hanging out in relentless people-pleasing has decreased. I'm quicker to hear the call of my inside self as it expresses a need or uncomfortable feeling. And I can allow those needs to count in ways I never before could. I can tell others the truth when I cannot help them at a particular time.

That's the beauty of building a connection with ourselves. It allows us to step into our imperfect humanness, where relief lives. Of course, our humanness was always there, but when the lens of wrongness guides us, it leaves little room for us to believe it's OK to have our own needs and uncomfortable feelings, or to show up imperfectly for others. Yet when we invite curiosity into the experience of people-pleasing, this enables us to wonder what our inside experience is, which restores a connection with our inner compass. And just like that, there's room for us to be human instead of perfect. Clarity, guidance and relief also slide in. All because we paused for a few micro-moments to come back home inside ourselves with curiosity.

Are you a people-pleaser or an emotional sponge? Do you often feel unappreciated? Do you question whether you're good enough? Do you run on fumes yet continue to tend to the needs of those around you? Well, guess what happens when you learn to take the most radical step in self-care, come back home to your inside self, and tune in to your *own* feelings even while taking care of others? You begin to feel lighter. Your energy increases. You laugh more. You're able to step back into the flow. You discover how to allow yourself to count too. And you see all the ways that the hard in life becomes easier.

The next time you find yourself in the throes of using your gifts to tend to the needs of those around you, take a quiet moment to keep it in balance. Turn your attention inward and tend to the feelings within you too. Simply notice them. Tune in to where you feel them in your body. Say hi to them if that feels comfortable.

See what you find. Many discover that their gifts ultimately expand as they practice this. You will certainly find that when you offer your gifts to the world *while* staying connected to your inside self, your gifts will lift *both* you and others up simultaneously. Best of all? You will be left feeling appreciated, loved, and taken care of because the most profound way we can feel this from others is if we give it to ourselves.

Chapter Twelve

RAGE ATTACKS AND OTHER CLUES THAT YOU'RE FAR FROM HOME

Oh, baby, there sure are a lot of ways to do anger. I've certainly used my fair share of approaches.

We had a paper route for many years when my middle sister and I were kids. Sometimes we had deep, adolescent talks about life while delivering the newspapers. Other times we argued like maniacs. As we walked to our route one particular day, we had a big argument, about what I no longer remember. I was sooooo mad at her. I sped ahead and hid off where she couldn't see me. As she approached, I jumped out and started throwing punches and kicking her. This was not my usual modus operandi, but I distinctly remember feeling convinced that physically expressing my rage would help drain it. So, I did. But as I hit her, I was stunned to notice that my rage only increased. I remember wondering if this is what many experience when physically abusing another person.

Another skill I've already alluded to is "going all New York" on people when they make me angry! I grew up in New York and certainly learned how to fight for my rights, whether it was dealing with a rude customer service representative, a challenging colleague, a patient's difficult family member, or a neighbor refusing to cut down a dead tree whose limbs were falling on my driveway. My "going all New York" approach was direct and sometimes confrontational, if needed. I spent years feeling proud of my ability to do this when the situation required it. It wasn't till years into this practice that I realized how much energy it took to pull this off each time. And I noticed that it didn't necessarily ease the feelings of anger at all but fed them instead.

While the silent treatment was one expression of anger I learned as a kid growing up in my house, rage was another one. My dad was an active alcoholic until I was ten, when he stopped drinking, but it was years before he went to AA (Alcoholics Anonymous). In those seven in-between years, he was what some refer to as a dry drunk. A dry drunk* is an alcoholic who no longer drinks but otherwise maintains the same behavior patterns of an alcoholic because they haven't dealt with the issues that caused them to become addicted in the first place. What did this look like? Anger, irritability, and yelling. He loudly banged pots and pans, yelling as he angrily yanked them out of the cabinets as he prepared to make dinner. His rages weren't daily but generally appeared when my mom was at work or out of the house.

The yelling and banging of pots and pans stressed me out. I hated the loudness of it all. But I never hung out in that stress for long because I routinely experienced an innate and immediate duty to shut my dad's rages down and protect my sisters, not from physical violence but verbal rage. And I was good at it. Really good. I learned how to get him to stop. It often involved me yelling and raging back at him and schooling him in whatever was not acceptable for that moment. And for whatever reason, he usually listened.

Back then, it never occurred to me that my dad's rages directly resulted from his alcoholism. I also didn't understand that his own lens of wrongness was driving them. I look back now and recognize that he didn't yet know how to use a

---

* https://www.webmd.com/mental-health/addiction/what-to-know-dry-drunk-syndrome

lens of curiosity to notice what he felt or needed. Instead, his unacknowledged feelings came out sideways.

My dad joined AA when I was a junior in high school, and he started to grow in entirely new ways. One morning before school, he stopped me in our upstairs hall to apologize for not being the dad we needed or wanted him to be, which confused me. I honestly didn't know what he was talking about because I didn't know it could be different. These periodic rages, followed by repeated apologies, were simply a part of our relationship with him. As he spoke, tears streamed down his face, which I'd never witnessed, and compelled me to reassure him that he didn't need to worry. But he insisted he intended to learn how to be a better father. And it turns out he wasn't kidding because he's gone on to be the most phenomenal, caring, engaged dad I could ever imagine having. While I can still recall his rages, they no longer hold a significant charge for me, which reminds me that our personal growth often has the power to heal in unexpected ways.

AND THEN RAGE CONSUMED ME!

Do you know who went on to rage at her kids years later? Me. Am I proud of this? Gosh, no. It's painful to look back and see this. It generally happened in the late afternoons and evenings when dinner and bedtime were approaching, when there were more demands with less time and energy to complete them. I'd regularly reach a breaking point when it didn't feel like they were listening or cleaning up after being asked. And my yelling would start. This relieved me momentarily because it released some of the building pressure inside me. And my yelling certainly got their attention, but it also did something else that I tried not to notice. It gave them the same eyes I know my sisters and I had each time my dad raged. A mix of fear, an immediate willingness to people-please, mistrust, and readiness to fight. Over time, I noticed something else. The relief my rages offered only lasted for minutes before the internal pressure again grew.

Leading up to these rages, my mind was using a lens of wrongness to scan my surroundings for anything and everything the kids were doing wrong or the ways the night wasn't going smoothly. My entire focus was outside me. I didn't yet know how to be curious about what I needed that I might be able to give myself in those moments. Instead, my mind searched for all the ways the kids took advantage of my role as a mom, and how so many responsibilities fell on my shoulders. But remember what happens when our lens of wrongness triggers all these stories in our minds. The stories end up locking our uncomfortable emotions within us, which is exactly what happened. And when these feelings are pinned down with no relief in sight, they build. And build. And then they come out sideways in an attempt to bring relief.

This is the cycle I moved through. How did my kids respond to these sideways rages of mine? Immediately, they became obedient, quickly cleaning up or doing whatever I asked. But over time, my rages showed them that this was how we communicated. It didn't help them learn to be better listeners. It didn't foster in them an increased sense of self-responsibility about cleaning up after themselves, whether it was toys, dishes, or dirty clothes. It simply taught them to react to screaming with whatever behavior would turn down the yelling.

But something changed when I discovered another side of my experience with anger. As I learned how to come back home to my body and emotions *in* the moment, I was surprised to find other feelings tucked beneath my rage. When anger shows up, our minds instinctively kick into focusing on what the other person has done to us, endlessly justifying all the reasons we have a right to be mad and further fueling our anger. We often have many physical sensations accompanying emotions like anger, but our minds prefer to stay busy thinking about the anger rather than feeling it.

As I applied my micro-moment pauses to my experience with anger, I often spent the first few minutes fuming inside about how I was justified in feeling the way I was feeling. My mind spun around and around with no relief in sight. But a bit into the pause, I remembered to check in with my body and notice where I was feeling sensations. There was tightness in my chest; I felt short of breath; my fists were clenched, as was my jaw; my heart was pounding. Each time, my mind continued to beckon me back to thinking about the story and my resulting anger. Still, I've repeatedly learned that when my mind stays stuck in the story, it locks those very emotions inside us and limits the possibility of relief. Instead, I continued to gently drop below the surface of my thinking to the physical sensations I was experiencing in the presence of my anger and rage.

I repeatedly discovered that I needed something I wasn't giving myself in that moment. Sometimes, I realized I was starving. Other times I'd been going full speed all day and needed ten minutes to rest before tackling dinner. And sometimes, I simply needed to verbalize that I was tired and crabby. I discovered that my rages were a way to avoid the uncomfortable emotions that sat beneath the yelling: feeling like my needs didn't count, feeling exhausted, feeling unheard, feeling hurt, feeling out of control, etc. In truth, this is true for all the different ways we learn to express anger, whether it's rage, the silent treatment, or another version altogether.

Over time, this practice enabled me to start pausing midrage to acknowledge what was happening inside me. Sometimes this meant saying to the kids, "Ugh, I know this doesn't feel good to you guys when I scream like this. It feels terrible to me too. I'm sorry I just screamed again. I want you to know that I'm working on finding a better way to express myself."

Each time I took those micro-moment pauses when my rage showed up, a shift occurred. As I returned home to my body, and my spinning mind slowed, space was created for clarity and relief to seep in in ways that weren't even conceivable a few minutes earlier.

Contrary to what our minds try to convince us when emotions like anger show up in our stories, they simply ask for acknowledgment from us. They want to be allowed rather than fought against. Their mere presence is a call from within, signaling us home. Clarity and relief become possible when we accept the invitation to drop below the surface of merely thinking about our anger and tune in to the embodied experience of feeling it *in* the moment.

This is something I have come to practice regularly in my life. Do I do it perfectly all the time? Nope! I'm as human as the next person. And the beauty of being human is that there's room for us to be imperfect, learn from our mistakes, grow, and repair important relationships. My daughter recently mentioned a chat with another kiddo's mom on the way home from soccer practice. She told this mom I used to yell a lot, but I don't anymore. She said, "Remember when you used to yell all the time, Mommy? You don't anymore!" And I realized how much I've changed. And how deeply grateful I am to understand the power of pausing in the micro-moment to come home to myself.

CHANGING THE CHANNEL IN THE FACE OF BIG FEELINGS

What about the times when it feels *impossible* to come back home to yourself in the face of big feelings? Do you ever wonder where the hell the rule book is when you're trying to figure out how to be a helpful parent or human in the face of hard feelings like anger? Here's the thing. We all have anger. And sometimes it can grow *really* big. I'll bet you know those moments I'm talking about.

Well, we had many of them in our house over the last few

years. My youngest daughter was in pre-K when the COVID pandemic hit. Her ability to express herself with words was still in its incubation stage. The world changed overnight. These changes were difficult for grown adults to make sense of, so you can imagine how confused her little mind was. Playdates shifted to the front lawn, with blankets over six feet apart from whatever friend was visiting. The imaginary play that had always involved physical interactions abruptly depended upon verbal expression only. Each time she or her friend tried to move closer to one another, the adults gently but firmly reminded them to return to their blankets. Fear sat crouched behind our grown-up words of guidance because there was so much we didn't yet know about COVID, which left us ever-mindful of the potential threat of serious illness and death.

She had video chats with her teachers and friends. She became a huge fan of the online exercise classes that she saw my wife and me doing during quarantine. This meant we often walked into the room to find her lifting tiny weights or copying the particular stretches and moves shown by the instructor on the screen, sometimes for twenty to thirty minutes! It's a COVID memory we will never forget, and it was an outlet she loved.

But there was another side to her experience. Her limited ability to express herself with words resulted in feelings lodged inside her little body with few ways out. This resulted in expressing herself more regularly through physical means. At first, we didn't think much of it. But as time went on, these physical expressions became pre-K-level rage attacks that involved kicking, punching, pinching, biting, and scratching. The tiniest frustration could trigger this many times a day. And these episodes lasted anywhere from ten to thirty minutes.

We encouraged her to notice what she felt, but this question only added to her frustration and overwhelm. I asked her where she felt the madness in her body. She didn't know.

I wondered aloud if she could draw her anger since she's an artist and loves to draw. She promptly drew a picture of her hands and colored them in dark red crayons. We taped a few copies of these hands around the house to help us remember to check in with her to see where in her body she was feeling the anger. This seemed like a step in a helpful direction, given that it allowed her to check inside herself about what she was feeling, even if it was simply the sensations of anger in her hands. But it didn't stop the rages. Oh, they just kept coming!

One afternoon, during a particular rage, I grabbed a big pillow and held it in front of my body. I told her to notice how much madness she had in her body and punch it into that pillow. I encouraged her as she punched that pillow and screamed her brains out. I told her it was great that she was letting that madness out. Her punches went on and on and on. At some point, I wondered exactly how long it might last, as twenty minutes had already passed. Another five minutes passed, and then she looked at me and said, "Can I stop now? I'm getting tired. Or should I keep going?" Oy. This was one of those moments when I'd wished for a handbook on how to effectively handle rage in my pre-K kid! She'd been ready to stop for a while, but she thought she needed to keep going for me. Oops! Needless to say, we stopped this pillow-punching session and got on with the afternoon. But I was still unsure how to help her navigate her intense frustration with more ease.

Around this time, my older daughter, now a tween, had a window of time when she felt notably angry and upset. Offers to talk about it weren't accepted. Nor were offers to snuggle or hug. All were met with cold, angry stares. I was utterly bewildered, thinking, "Shit, how the hell do I handle this?" One evening, as we navigated another round of this at around 10:30 p.m., I heard myself saying aloud, "Well, you don't want a hug, and you don't want to talk about it. Do you wanna race instead?" As soon as I said it, I thought, "What the hell, Emily? Race?" But my daughter immediately perked up and said, "Ok, race how?" And again, I heard myself saying, "Get your shoes on (she was already in her pajamas). We're hitting the street. Get ready for your mom to beat your butt up that hill outside!"

Of course, she guffawed at the idea that I could beat her in a race, but she wasn't taking into account that I had a newfound love for running that COVID quarantine created! We headed out into the night and sprinted up and down the street we live on, tackling the giant hill numerous times. I'll admit that she and I were *both* surprised by my impressive speed! After about ten minutes of sprint-racing and laughing, we plopped down on some stairs in front of a nearby apartment complex. There was a little more space for us to chat. Her feelings could come out as the real deal rather than all wrapped up in a big, confusing, angry reaction.

Did this unconventional outing fix the issues at hand? Nah. There was still more to work out. The issue showed up again for the next few nights. But did our unexpected nighttime race create some space for the feelings to be there without us having to work hard to fix them? Yes! Did it lessen the seriousness that happens when big feelings show up and we become hell-bent on getting them to go away? Yup.

If it sounds like I'm suggesting that the answer is to go out sprinting into the night when you have big feelings, let me assure you I'm not. It's not specifically *what* my daughter and I did that night that was the most helpful, although it *was* fun! It was that we changed the channel. And sometimes, that's the most valuable thing we can do.

Big feelings like anger often compel us to stare intensely into the eyes of those feelings, thinking harder and harder about them and how to find the solutions or how to make the feelings go away. And it's not just the person *having* the feelings. Parents and others around that person can easily feel pulled to do this about the other person's big feelings too.

But you know what frequently happens when we respond

this way? It makes us feel worse. Our shoulders move up by our ears. Maybe our jaw tightens. Or our neck starts to hurt. And our big feelings become bigger. Before we know it, our thinking mind begins to take these big feelings and generalize them to many other areas of our life. And then we have *really big* feelings. This is such a human experience.

My nighttime racing adventure with my daughter was a helpful reminder to me. Not just about how to help her, but my younger daughter too. It reawakened something I already knew but had forgotten in the face of my kiddos' anger and frustration: It isn't about trying to fix or get rid of their big, uncomfortable feelings. Sometimes it's about acknowledging that they're here. And then changing the channel for a stint.

Big feelings don't always need to be worked out quickly to feel relief. Sometimes, when the intensity of a feeling grows, it can be helpful to change the channel for a bit. Instead of working harder to find the fixes, change the channel, and do something else entirely. This creates more space for the big feelings to emerge as the real deal rather than all wrapped up in a big, confusing reaction.

What are some channel changers? Well, sometimes it might be journaling about your feelings rather than just thinking about them in your head. Maybe it's going for a walk or run. Perhaps it's throwing yourself into painting, drawing, or coloring. Sometimes it's reading or listening to a novel that carries you into a different life or world. Maybe it's sitting out in nature with your bare feet on the ground while noticing how many colors, sounds, animals, trees, and plants you can notice. The channel-changing possibilities are endless. For my youngest, it turns out the *best* channel changer is when I act terrified of the evil eye she gives me when she's angry! This immediately results in fits of uncontrollable laughter from her so she can return to her anger with a broader perspective, a bit more levity, and an ever-growing ability to verbally, instead of physically, express her big feelings.

Anger is one of those big feelings we navigate as humans. Sometimes we find relief when we come back home inside ourselves amidst our anger and notice what we're feeling and needing. And sometimes, this feels impossible. Does it mean you're doing it wrong when this happens? Nope. Instead, it's simply a clue that a different way is needed right then. And intentionally changing the channel in those moments can be monumentally helpful.

Here's the deal. Everywhere we look, we can find things in our lives that can trigger big feelings like anger. And sometimes, changing the channel is the kindest move you can make to create relief for yourself in the middle of the triggers.

Where in your life are the big feelings like anger and rage showing up? How have you learned to express those emotions: with silence, rage, yelling, throwing, etc? Is your particular expression of it working well for you and those around you? If yes, woohooo! But if not, maybe it's time for a slow and steady update to a new approach. If it feels easy to come back home inside yourself amid your anger and notice what you're feeling or needing, great! But if that feels impossible, don't make yourself wrong about it. Instead, see what happens when you momentarily change the channel instead. This may just create the space inside you that leads to surprising relief amid your big feelings and allows you to circle back to those feelings with more perspective and a renewed ability to talk about it. Give it a try and see what you find. And if your channel change ends up being a nighttime sprint race, you *know* I'll want to hear about it!

Chapter Thirteen

UNSPOKEN ANGER

The silent treatment was an approach I spent *years* refining in the face of anger, and wow, was I good at becoming silent but fuming. You may know this approach, too, whether it's one you use or one that's been used on you. It's interesting how often silent treatment is used in families. In fact, it's often an approach that's passed down from generation to generation as it was in my family. It's a momentarily effective way to navigate anger or hurt because it doesn't require the use of words, nor does it ask us to be direct with the other person about our feelings or have the hard conversations that are often necessary to repair a relationship or work out a conflict. My best friend from high school *still* remembers the ten days I stopped talking with her simply because she'd made a no-longer-remembered comment that made me momentarily mad. Sadly, I ended numerous friendships this way over the years and inevitably moved on from anger to regret, yet it was usually too late to remedy the friendships.

Whether you give the silent treatment, or it's being done to you, the lens of wrongness quietly slips in and impacts the stories you tell yourself. What do I mean by this? Well, notice how your mind spins with the details of an interaction that led to the silent treatment. Whether you are the giver or receiver of the silence doesn't matter. You are either repeating the story of what happened or noticing how the other person wronged you, thus justifying your silence. Or you're repeatedly reviewing your last interactions with the person giving you the silent treatment, convinced you must have done something wrong to cause it. And in this case, your mind likely comes up with all kinds of guesses about how you were wrong to explain the other person's silence. You might even feel a hot wave of shame move through you as you identify yet another thing you said or did that could be to blame.

I've come to understand that giving the silent treatment is a great way to avoid feeling your emotions in those micro-moments. It really is. The silent treatment enables you to cut off from your emotions and kick into matter-of-fact mode. Maybe you know this mode. It's when you become notably matter-of-fact about an experience that triggered a strong feeling in you. Instead, it becomes an intellectual exercise. Back in the day, when the silent treatment was my primary way to navigate anger, this matter-of-fact mode was intricately woven into my experience. When someone's words hurt or pissed me off, I immediately acted like I didn't care about this person. The mantra, "Act like you don't care," circled through my head all day long. But the only way I could do this was to cut off from the raw, real feelings beneath my silence. My focus remained on the other person's wrongness, and my silence was a way to make them pay for how they wronged me. But do you notice how my silence and this focus on the other person's wrongness prevented me from making room for my feelings of hurt, betrayal, or other uncomfortable emotions that sat just below my anger? The silent treatment became a way to banish not only the other person but my own feelings too.

When I started attending Al-Anon meetings in my early twenties, my view and use of the silent treatment underwent a notable update. Before Al-Anon, I was proud of my ability to "remain tough" and cut someone out with silence. I focused on what the other person had done to me and acted like I wasn't bothered that I wasn't talking with them. But there was another reality under the surface: I was freaking out on the inside. My silence didn't do anything to stop my spiraling thoughts as I went over the story's details, always trying to prove to myself that I was right. The silence also didn't ease my feelings of anger, hurt, or shame. Instead, it further fueled those emotions and created no room to repair the relationship. Al-Anon taught me that the silent treatment was a way to avoid using my words or being direct and honest about how I felt.

But I discovered I often didn't know what I felt beneath my anger and silence because it was always accompanied by my matter-of-fact mode and lens of wrongness. And this allowed me to avoid feeling those emotions like hurt and grief. However, something changed as Al-Anon taught me to take my focus off another person and place it back on myself. At first, it was so hard to shift my focus from what the other person had done to me. But each time I brought my focus back home inside me, sometimes for mere micro-moments in the beginning, I felt a flash of relief. And it became increasingly possible to notice those emotions beneath my anger and silence.

Did this mean my use of the silent treatment stopped? Not exactly. Initially, I didn't even realize I was doing the silent treatment until I was already deep in it. After a while, it became possible to notice the presence of my silent treatment halfway through, and I'd pause to tune in to what I was feeling. My mind always wanted to harness my lens of wrongness and review the stories that reflected how the other person had wronged me. But I repeatedly found this only cemented my need to maintain my silence toward them. It was only when I invited a lens of curiosity that relief quietly slipped in. More clarity and understanding invariably moved in when I became curious about what I was feeling beneath my anger and silence.

Over time, it became possible to communicate with others more directly. Oy, it was scary as hell in the beginning. My whole body trembled as I approached anyone to talk about how I felt, whether it was anger, hurt, or another feeling. But you know what I found? Most were surprised by my directness, and many were initially uncomfortable. But the conversations that followed often became heartfelt and invited growth and healing that we both appreciated. Innumerable relationships of mine deepened as I practiced this directness because it invited us to step forward with honesty and a lens of curiosity. And it turns out these are integral to fostering healthy, meaningful relationships.

When Silence Hurts

My baby sister, one of my best friends in the entire world, and one of the people I trusted the most in the universe, abruptly stopped talking to me eighteen years ago. After nearly daily phone calls with her for years, her unforeseen silence utterly confused me. My lens of wrongness went full-court press as my mind relentlessly reviewed our prior conversations and interactions, searching for my wrongness to explain her silence. I spent endless months and years coming up with possible stories that would help make sense of this experience, convinced I'd done something wrong to lead her to cut me out of her life.

But here's the tricky part I've learned since those early days of silence. In *both* scenarios, whether we're giving or receiving the silent treatment, those stories further fuel our uncomfortable emotions and cement them inside us. They don't allow for relief, even if the thinking is our mind's attempt to gain relief. Why is this? Because the stories prevent us from *feeling* the unwelcome, often painful emotions that sit beneath the stories. As my mind generated stories about my sister's silence and my assumed wrongness, it prevented me from experiencing my incredible grief and anger in embodied ways. Instead, the stories created an intellectual experience of those emotions. But an academic experience of emotions makes true relief impossible to attain. The silent treatment also involves no communication with the other person using words, making the possible repair of the relationship almost unreachable.

Many of us know this experience of being on the giving or receiving end of the silent treatment. It's a real way that many learn to navigate anger. And it's stunning how integrally a lens of wrongness is woven into this. As the years of silence from my beloved sister have climbed onward, my lens of wrongness continues to show up as it's such a common, default human lens. There are many times when I don't even realize it's here as my mind reviews the stories of what I may have done wrong or of how wrong she is to be silent.

I continually learn that my lens of wrongness is simply an attempt to protect me from having to feel my incredible grief of missing the hell out of my sister and the hurt about her silence. And it's likely the same for you, too, whether you are the giver or receiver of silence. Sure, your feelings may not be grief or hurt, but if silence is present, this suggests uncomfortable feelings are likely lurking too. And when we're using a lens of wrongness, it locks those emotions within us so they can't move, which means no genuine relief is in sight.

When I catch myself using this lens and shift to one of curiosity, it invites me back inside, where it's possible to notice those feelings tucked beneath the stories. When I see my sadness and hurt sitting there, it enables me to acknowledge them and be present with these periodic roommates, even for a few micro-moments. And I feel relief. Is it the kind of relief that makes my grief and hurt go away? Nah. But it stops me from fighting against their presence. It eliminates the denial that those emotions are here. And those unwelcome roommates named Grief and Hurt feel acknowledged, and they experience my presence, which is what they'd been needing all along. But the most surprising and beautiful result is something else entirely. I move from *only* being able to feel confusion, anger, grief, and hurt to *simultaneously* feeling bottomless love for my sister, compassion for our journey through this human lens of wrongness, and curiosity about how we will one day connect again.

The truth is that my default reaction *still* surfaces sometimes in my life, so I instinctively *want* to kick into the silent treatment when I feel angry or hurt with someone. But I've learned that my lens of wrongness invariably shows up in those moments. And it turns out it's far more helpful to shift my focus from these stories of wrongness about what the other person did. Instead, I invite a lens of curiosity as I focus inward and notice the feelings *inside* me. Is it hurt, sadness, fury, etc.?

I drop my focus from my mind into my body and notice the sensations accompanying my emotions. I make space for these feelings and sensations in this micro-moment. Sometimes I do this briefly, and then clarity about the next helpful steps arrives. Other times, I only pause for a few seconds at a time throughout the day, noticing how I'm feeling inside because any more than that feels intolerable. Over time, as I apply this lens of curiosity to those micro-moments of anger and silence, my tolerance for those emotions increases and greater insight slips in. It becomes possible to discern whether I need to speak directly with the other person about how I'm feeling or if simply befriending my emotions on the inside will offer that relief and healing. A shift from a lens of wrongness to one of curiosity again leads to relief that our minds are convinced isn't possible.

RESENTMENT CAN KILL YOU
OR MAKE YOU STRONGER

Resentment is another common way many of us learn to express our anger silently, and, oh baby, was I good at becoming silent but seething with resentment.

It's so easy for resentment to quickly consume your mind. And the more you think about it, the more proof you find that you're justified in feeling how you do. It's certainly harder to feel close to the person you resent, which sometimes leads to wondering why you're even in a relationship with them.

The more resentful you feel, the less you use your words to directly say what you feel, let alone need. Instead, it comes out sideways. You sigh with frustration when you're around the other person. You clench your jaw and look annoyed in the hope that they'll respond in some way. Perhaps you cry, trying to get them to notice your feelings. Maybe you blow up about other issues that have nothing to do with the original resentment. You may slam pots and pans into the cabinet a little too hard as you're putting them away. Or you quietly discuss with friends or strangers how peeved you are, but you don't mention it to the person triggering your peeved state. Do you notice how wordless *and* powerless you feel throughout this? Yeah, I've noticed too.

In the first few years of my marriage, this resentful part of me showed up rather regularly. I grew up with an innate feeling that I always needed to be busy doing, fixing, or solving things until I got everything right. I was convinced that I could finally relax once I got it all perfect. But when you hold this perspective, you *never* stop finding more things that need to be done, fixed, or solved, which means the rest never comes.

My wife, on the other hand, has a natural ability to rest when she's tired or under the weather. She even rests simply to rest! When I first encountered this alien behavior of hers, I was so confused by it. And then I started to resent it. Why could she take time out to rest when I was still working so hard on things? And before I knew it, I'd find even more to work on, which further fueled my resentment. I know *now* that her ability to rest is a true gift, and her once alien behavior now inspires me, but I sure didn't see it that way in our early days together.

It's painful to remember how I handled my resentment when our youngest was born. I gave birth to our oldest daughter in Seattle, while my wife delivered her little sister four years later after we relocated to North Carolina. My wife was pregnant when we moved, so we were careful not to have her carry the heavy moving boxes, etc. I wish I could say I felt all loving and caring about this, but I'll admit I often didn't. I was annoyed that it all landed on me. As is common with pregnancy, my wife hit windows of time when she felt completely worn out and needed to lie down and rest. Is this to be expected? Hell yeah! But I'm embarrassed to admit that her resting wholeheartedly bothered me.

Fast-forward to the months after our youngest daughter's birth. Let's just say my resentment didn't exactly recede, nor did my lens of wrongness. Instead, they went from a simmer to a boil. All my mind could focus on was everything in the house and the family I was managing, and how wrong it was. No matter how much I tried to remind myself that my wife was dealing with all that comes with a newborn, including the massive hormone changes and nursing, I couldn't shake this growing resentment that I was the one handling everything else.

Of course, at that time, I didn't fume directly to her about this. Instead, I stomped around, pissed and silent, muttering aggravated phrases under my breath when she passed me. Until one particular night, I no longer recall the specific topic. I remember feeling angry and resentful as she asked me to step outside in the dark driveway, away from our kids, to talk for a minute. I heard a curious sound and looked up to realize she was sobbing. It turns out she'd felt my endless, indirect guilt trips for months, and they'd worn her down. She argued that she also contributed to the family's needs and pointed out the many ways.

Well, folks, this put me in a tricky spot. There I was, boiling with resentment toward this person I love and adore. And I felt justified in this feeling. Yet seeing my love, who'd delivered our second baby only a few months before, sobbing because of the impact of my behavior? Well, that utterly sucked and left me feeling both resentful *and* guilty. But this conversation ultimately birthed actual communication about how we'd both been feeling. It invited direct words into the experience as well as a lens of curiosity.

Through further discussions, we decided to write down a list of the responsibilities we each handled. We shared these lists and found different aspects of the other's list eye-opening. It allowed us to review the lists and decide who would be captain on which tasks going forward. It enabled us to pick responsibilities we each felt a greater affinity toward. I became captain of dishes and laundry. My wife became captain of folding the clean laundry and taking out the trash. On we went, divvying up the household tasks this way. This brought me incredible relief because tucked beneath all my resentment was a need for more structure and clarity about our duties. But when I focused on my bitterness, it kept me stuck in believing that I had to put others' needs before mine. That's what resentment does! It steals our power and leaves us feeling we don't count—and consequently makes our needs wrong.

We continue to use this tool to divvy up household responsibilities. I look back on that period when our youngest was a newborn and am so grateful for the gifts that experience ended up giving me. It was the first time I learned to navigate resentment with a lens of curiosity, and it brought relief. It led me to discover, yet again, that my resentment hadn't been wrong. And that my wife hadn't been wrong either! My resentment was simply a clue to me that I was needing something. It invited me to become more curious about what those needs were and how I might be able to have those needs met.

RESENTMENT BECOMES A CLUE

Direct communication about my resentment was the first step in creating a different experience. But my dance with bitterness transformed even more when I learned how to be present *in* my body instead of just my mind when I was feeling resentful. Yeah, it's worth reading that sentence again. As my mind harnessed my lens of wrongness, it wanted to keep my focus out there on my wife and her behavior. But my body had something else to say. It was asking me to slow down and take a break. It was beckoning me back home. Coming back into my body *while* feeling resentful allowed me to see parts of the equation I'd never before noticed: no one forced me to keep working so hard without a break. No one except *me*!

I was reminded of this when my resentment reappeared at home, but this time toward my kiddos. For a while, I assumed this was a necessary part of momming. And it's true, as caregivers, there are endless times when we're asked to keep giving when it feels like we have nothing left. And that's exactly what I assumed was happening as I worked tirelessly to keep up with the dishes in our house. Kids have an innate gift for generating pounds of dishes each day. And as the captain of dishes in our house, these pounds of dishes were my responsibility.

For a while, I wallowed in my resentment, quietly feeling sorry for myself. But things changed when I remembered to invite in curiosity. I dropped from all the thinking in my mind down into my body. I noticed it felt like a heavy weight was sitting on my shoulders every night when I unloaded the clean dishes from the dishwasher. I could hardly stand every second of that task. Interestingly, I noticed my shoulders *didn't* feel heavy when I loaded the dishwasher with dirty dishes. In fact, loading the dirty dishes left me feeling accomplished! This brought curiosity into the mix. It also ushered in clarity about what I was needing. I realized that emptying the *clean* dishes triggered resentment in me. This led me to recognize that my kids were old enough to participate in household duties like this. My wife and I asked them to be captain of emptying the clean dishwasher each night, while I continued to be captain of the dirty dishes. And I felt so much better!

Hot damn, look what my resentment led me to! But it

wasn't until I shifted to a lens of curiosity that this became possible. It enabled me to drop below the surface of all the thinking about my resentment and tune in to the experience in my body *during* it. New understanding dawned and my resentment took on an entirely new meaning. Instead of it being about what someone else was doing that was unfair or wrong to me, my resentment became a clue that I needed something I wasn't getting. And it invited me to become curious about this need and how I might have it met.

Our lens of wrongness can so easily slip into our experience with resentment so that we can only see possible solutions in an all-or-nothing, black-or-white way. Yet when we invite ourselves to come down from our spinning, fuming minds and into our bodies, this ushers in curiosity. There's instantly space to wonder what we're needing in that moment. And to ponder if there's a way we can give ourselves the very thing we need but in a different way than our minds envision.

Over the years, I've learned I can use my words to directly tell my wife or anyone else when I feel resentful. Wild, huh? It doesn't mean they have to fix it. I started saying to my wife, "Honey, I'm feeling so freakin' resentful right now. I want to blame you, but I need time to sit with it and figure out what I need. I don't need you to fix it. I just want you to know why I'm acting this way and that I'm working on figuring it out. And I'll let you know when I have more clarity."

The strangest thing happened when I started doing this. My wife didn't have to guess what I was feeling anymore. And it made me feel less "victimy". It made me curious to understand what I was needing. It made me realize I could frequently give myself what I needed in a way that I believed only my wife could give me when I was swimming in resentment. Directly using my words, even to express my resentment, softened the very experience of it.

A different experience becomes possible with just about

anything when we invite a shift from using a lens of wrongness to one of curiosity. A lens of wrongness naturally triggers our minds to generate stories that pin our uncomfortable feelings in place. These stories convince us there are only one or two possible solutions to the situation and they both usually suck! But when a lens of curiosity is engaged, it allows us to pause, settle into our bodies, and become present enough to notice what we're feeling and needing. It enables words to become part of the mix, whether about our silent anger or unspoken resentment. And the chance for our needs to be met goes up exponentially because, contrary to what our lens of wrongness routinely tries to convince us, *we* often have the power to give ourselves what we've been needing all along.

Chapter Fourteen

WHAT IF IT'S TIME TO UPDATE YOUR STORY?

When I first learned of my daughter's dyslexia, the news triggered a cascade of feelings in me. My wife and I sat with the testing specialist as she reviewed her findings, and I found myself pushing down sobs that threatened to escape from my throat. Later, we met with the teachers and her tutor to discuss the newest findings and develop a plan. I again found myself suppressing sobs and averting my eyes as they repeatedly brimmed with tears. After that meeting, I climbed into our car directly outside the school's front doors, waiting for my wife and kids to come out. Students and parents flooded past me for end-of-day pickup while I hyperventilated in that car. It had been thirty years since I'd last hyperventilated.

I was confused by my reaction. I experienced the news of my daughter's dyslexia as if she'd received a death sentence. I had been diagnosed with what we'd called "learning problems" forty-five years earlier. Even the phrase "learning problems" or learning disabilities suggests an inherent wrongness. The unseen story I'd told myself about my learning style all those years ago came pouring into my awareness. I discovered my story revolved around the wrongness of my learning differences with the wrongness of me tucked beneath that. You can guess how stories like this feel! Not only are they disempowering, but they also limit our very sense of possibility and hope while moving through an experience.

The stories we tell ourselves matter. Half the time, we don't even realize we're telling ourselves one. Stories allow our minds to make sense of our experiences, feelings, and the world around us. We need stories for this reason, but which stories we land on can profoundly impact how we feel as we move through any experience.

Here's the catch, though: *We can't choose a different story if we don't realize the current one isn't serving us.* Becoming aware of my own story of wrongness, born all those years ago, ultimately made room for a different story to dawn. My daughter's diagnosis of dyslexia led me to uncover the story I'd embodied and told myself for forty-five years regarding my learning differences. And it turned out it had never served me.

As I wondered how to help my daughter create a more empowering story for herself, I became curious about how I wanted to feel about my unique learning style. This led me to an updated story that made room for the incredible gifts that showed up as a result. I realized my learning style includes grit, determination and creative, outside-the-box thinking and perspectives. I moved into a deep understanding that there is no wrong way to learn. I started telling a new story that serves me far better and allows me to step into and own the intelligence that has always been mine. My new perspective holds a deep appreciation for how my unique approach to learning has so beautifully colored and shaped my world and experiences throughout my life. My daughter's dyslexia gave me the gift of an updated story.

I pondered how to help my daughter find a story about her dyslexia that would provide an understanding and appreciation for the unique way her brain is wired to see the world. I shared with her that she has a gift called dyslexia and that one of the things this means is that she can see in 3D. Did you know that research has found that those with dyslexia often have an ability to see in 3D? I explained that she can see letters, numbers, and other things from the front and the back, which can sometimes make reading, writing, or math tricky if she doesn't know when her superpower is on and when it's off. I outlined our intention to find tools and support to help her learn when it's on and off as this would make it easier for her to benefit from her superpower without feeling so frustrated. We wondered together about all the possible ways she will be able to apply this beautiful gift to her life.

Can you feel the difference between the story of wrongness I once told myself about my learning differences and this new story that my daughter began to tell? Each profoundly impacts our experience and feelings, although in notably divergent directions.

What are the stories in your life that hold your focus right now? Are they empowering? Do they help you feel a sense of possibility and hope about your experience? Is there another story to be told that might change your very experience with whatever challenge you're navigating? These are questions I've learned to ask myself. I don't always remember right away. Sometimes I find myself in the middle of an experience before being reminded. There was a time in my life when I didn't know my stories might impact my experiences. I didn't even know stories were being told! Once I discovered their presence, though, it tapped me into new possibilities.

What I do know is that despite how often my brain tries to convince me that there is only one way to see a situation and one story to tell, there are, in fact, many possible stories and perspectives, and the ones we choose to focus on really do influence the very experiences we have.

THE STORIES WE TELL OTHERS

We've all got things about ourselves we don't like. Sometimes it's our physical appearance, something about our personality, our emotions, or even our health. Have you ever noticed that the more you focus on it, the worse it feels, and the more you want to find a way to fix that part of you?

When I was an adolescent going through puberty, I grew five inches in one year. I promptly lost any lingering baby fat, exposing a long, narrow chin, a small chest, and a notably slender body. Others around me were fast developing curves, larger breasts, etc. As often happens in puberty, I developed a newfound preoccupation with these physical traits of mine. I felt ashamed and was sure others were noticing these "flaws" in me too.

I quickly learned to use humor to offset my shame. I joked with others that I sharpened my chin every day. I cupped my chin with one hand and turned an imaginary pencil sharpener with the other hand to depict how the sharpening was executed. I joked that I was built like my dad when I referenced my smaller chest size. Yeah, everybody laughed, and so did I. Over time, though, I noticed that when others joined me in joking about these traits of mine, I felt uneasy inside and even hurt. Yet clearly, I was sending the message that it was OK to joke about it.

I've heard others joke this way endless times too. I've encountered many who struggle with weight and frequently joke about their size. Their jokes tend to result in chuckles from them and others around them. What about those experiences when we don't understand something being taught to us, and we refer to ourselves as stupid? Or when we feel insecure about something we're navigating in life, and we quickly call ourselves idiots for not knowing what to do or how to handle it?

It seems so innocuous on the surface. We're simply trying to beat people to the punch because we anticipate it will make it hurt less if we joke about it first. Does it work, though? I have yet to meet someone for whom it does. Yes, using self-deprecating words to joke about the parts of ourselves we feel ashamed of certainly sends a clear message to others that it's acceptable for them to joke about it too. But what message is it sending to our bodies and feelings?

I remember reaching a point in high school when I noticed how much my insides cringed when others joined me in the jokes about my chin, smaller chest size, or body shape. It felt downright painful if they brought up the jokes without my initiation. There came a day when I decided to stop joking about any of it myself because I realized it simply permitted others to do the same. Wow, was that a strange transition. I was surprised to realize how often I felt inclined to joke about it all. Like, a lot. The thoughts would pop into my head, and I would almost blurt them out, but I would stop myself. It took practice, but my perspective shifted over time; strangely, I could feel my sweet chin, slender body, and small chest appreciate my new approach. I began to feel we were on the same team, rather than me fighting against what they were.

Words are powerful. We're constantly inundated with messages from a culture that promotes a lens of wrongness. This culture tells us there's a correct way to look, feel, act, and be. Part of our human experience will always be learning how to navigate between the messages we take in from the outside world and the messages we receive from our inside world. It's a dance. Sometimes the dance is beautiful, and sometimes it's not as graceful. The more we find ways to make our bodies and feelings our dance partners, the more room we create for a different experience with the traits we dislike about ourselves. How do we do this? By shifting from a lens of wrongness into one of curiosity, so we can notice the words and stories we use daily to describe ourselves. This invites us to spot how frequently we feel pulled to use self-deprecating comments about our looks, smarts, personality, etc. It can be surprising to note how it feels inside when we reference ourselves in these ways.

Does this mean there's no longer room for any humor about ourselves? Nah. I'd be in trouble if that were the case!

There's *always* room for humor. Instead, it's about harnessing curiosity so we can be honest with ourselves about how the use of that humor feels to each of us on the inside in a given moment or on a particular subject. When we disregard the feeling of unease, hurt, or even a sensation of cringing inside, this insidiously sends a message to our bodies and selves that we don't care about them or that they don't matter to us. Is that what we're trying to do in those moments? It likely is not, yet it's still the result.

I've written about how it changes our experience when we turn toward our emotions to meet them rather than fight against them. The same is true for our bodies. When we tune in to how the words and stories we use make our bodies and selves feel inside, this sends a clear message to them that we are a team and that they matter to us. This creates space for a different relationship to form with the parts of ourselves we were convinced were wrong and needed fixing. How cool is that?

When Stories Pin Unwanted Feelings in Place

During my recovery from thyroid cancer, I experienced muscle wasting. I frequently found myself down on the floor playing with my kids and unable to get back up without help from someone else. And if someone else wasn't available, it often resulted in rather humorous scenes that involved a lot of grunting and wild body maneuvering as I attempted to find some kind of position that allowed me to inch my way back into standing. I'm sure any video of this would result in chuckles from anyone who knows me because I already have a flair for physical humor, so you can bet my attempts to stand were performed in true Emily-esque style!

As the months progressed, I spent a lot of time focused on

this story about my muscle wasting. I thought about it all the time. My mind's lens of wrongness took over and endlessly reviewed the cause of my weakness. A story continued to circle through my mind, telling me this weakness was permanent now that my thyroid was gone. When I used the term muscle wasting with a friend one day, she commented that the term felt so hopeless. Hearing this pissed me off. I mean, it was a reality! Yet as I allowed her comment to percolate, I noticed the hopelessness that the term and story triggered in me. It felt so hopeless that I felt paralyzed to move forward with exercise to address it.

It's interesting how quietly a thought, word, or story can begin to tune us into an underlying feeling that can create an experience we never intended. There I was, marching around thinking, focusing, and talking about my muscle wasting, having no idea it was just one particular story available on this subject. I noticed that tucked beneath my reference to my muscle wasting was a suggestion of wrongness, as if my muscles were somehow betraying me and no longer on my team. Yet, if there is one thing I have repeatedly learned through my own experience and that of patients over the years, it is that our bodies do not betray us. Do they always function the way we hoped? Definitely not. I've also learned that there is never only one perspective available when trying to make sense of why our bodies are expressing difficult symptoms. It's so human for us to feel betrayed when our bodies seem to go renegade on us. Confusion, anger, and hopelessness are all very appropriate reactions. Making space for these feelings is so important. When we make space for our feelings of the present moment, purposefully acknowledge their presence, soften to them, and notice where we experience these emotions in our bodies, we begin to open the door to new perspectives on the very situations we're in.

A different perspective quietly slipped in when I began to notice, acknowledge, and allow that I was feeling hopeless and wrong regarding my muscle wasting. My mind unexpectedly offered a new term: "Hero Muscles," and I immediately felt the difference. It instantly placed my muscles on my team again, and I understood they always had been. I was flooded with love and appreciation for their unending willingness and eagerness to keep showing up and to become strong again when given the appropriate tools.

My hero muscles and I embarked on an inspired, empowering journey to become strong again. We joined Livestrong, a program through the YMCA that helps those who've gone through cancer rebuild strength. My muscles and I learned to use machines at the gym that we'd never before been one bit interested in. We (because we are a team, after all!) eagerly headed to the gym to stretch, build, and grow throughout the week, and it felt *so good*! Each day we noticed small, powerful shifts in the direction we wanted to go.

I once heard Elijah Cummings, a former US representative, say that when bad things happened to his kids, he taught them to ask not "Why is this happening to me?" but "How is this happening *for* me?" I spent several months unknowingly asking myself why my experience with side effects like muscle wasting was happening *to* me. When my friend suggested that the term muscle wasting felt hopeless, it felt like a direct challenge to a story that felt so undeniably true, which is why her comment initially pissed me off. Yet look at all the gifts I received through my muscle-wasting adventure as my broader understanding of it expanded when I shifted from a lens of wrongness to curiosity! It ultimately ignited an awareness that the feeling of betrayal by my body had once again come for a visit and was asking to be acknowledged by me. As I made room for the presence of this feeling, new, more empowering stories showed up that changed my relationship with my sweet hero muscles and my body and the process in which we found ourselves.

Does it make you curious about other ways your unwelcome

experiences may be happening *for* you rather than to you? Or what other stories might show up as you shift to a lens of curiosity and consider this? I've come to ask myself regularly how things could be happening for me. It repeatedly invites me to notice my current story and open to a more empowering one when needed.

WHEN ANXIETY DRIVES YOUR STORIES

Ooooh eeeeh, do stories complicate things for us when they're being driven by anxiety and worry. You know those nights when you're lying in bed, attempting to sleep, and the worry creeps in? All it takes is one thought to start the worry cascade. "Shit. How should I handle that situation? Are they gonna think I don't know what I'm doing? Why did Sara look at me that way when we were talking? It looked like she didn't like what I was suggesting. Oh, God, maybe I pissed her off. Why did I tell her that?" And then you replay the conversations or situations over and over, going over every detail, mapping out how to fix things or handle them differently.

Does this review of the stories and all the details bring relief as you're lying there stressing? Nope. Does your mind know this? Not at all. Your mind is convinced it's helping. What does your mind do when it isn't able to give you relief about the current concerns? It begins to scan your life for other things to focus on. The challenge is that your mind is using a lens of wrongness to do so, which means it easily identifies more areas of your life it deems wrong and in need of fixing. Perhaps it's your kids or your partner. Your mind abruptly reminds you that they might get hurt or die or that you can't keep them safe. Maybe the headache you've been navigating could be a brain tumor. Maybe it's your to-do list that feels insurmountable as you increasingly doubt your ability to get it all done or to do it well. Before you know it, you're convinced you're a bad mom, partner, employee, or even human.

Still, there's no relief in sight. This was my experience for eons. These anxiety-driven stories will never be able to offer us relief because they are simply the mind's way of trying to distract us from what's really at play: the presence of uncomfortable emotions. Remember when I mentioned there's a big difference between thinking about a feeling and feeling it? Well, stories are our mind's way of thinking about an unwanted feeling in an attempt to protect us from having to feel it. See? Our mind is on our side. Its intentions are truly good. It's trying to protect us in the only way it knows—with thinking! That's our mind's specialty. But all the thinking and ruminating about the stories only pins those emotions in place, making relief unattainable.

Here's an interesting thing about our stories, especially those driven by anxiety: there's often a theme running through them. Sure, on the surface, it can feel like a billion different themes to sift through as the various stories flood your awareness. But when you shift from a lens of wrongness to one of curiosity, you begin to notice there are underlying feelings tucked beneath each story. It's often the same unwanted feeling, despite the seemingly different stories.

You might think: *How should I handle that situation? They're gonna think I don't know what I'm doing!* There's an underlying fear of handling the situation the wrong way or having others see you aren't enough or are wrong, creating a threat of disconnection from others involved. *Why did Sara look at me that way when we were talking? It looked like she didn't like what I was suggesting. Oh, God, maybe I pissed her off. Why did I tell her that?* Notice the fear that you've handled your interaction poorly or wrong and that your wrongness will be visible to Sara or others, running the risk that a disconnect will form between you and Sara. *What if my kids are injured or die? What if I can't keep them safe?* Again, there's an underlying fear that you can't mother well enough or that you'll somehow do it wrong, resulting in ultimate separation from them. *What if my headaches mean I have a brain tumor?* There's the fear of separation through death. *I'm never gonna get everything on my to-do list done, let alone done well. Just more proof that I'm a bad mom, partner, employee, human.* Again, here is the fear that you can't do things right enough, leaving the threat that you will be rejected by others and experience a separation from them. This theme of wrongness and not-enoughness weaves its way through each story. And just beneath these fears lies the ultimate fear of separation from others because of your wrongness.

I can't tell you what the fears and feelings are beneath *your* stories, but your curiosity can help you uncover this. What I can guarantee is that unwanted fears and emotions *are* sitting beneath the varied stories your mind ruminates over. And inviting yourself to become curious about this is a gateway to relief.

How Curiosity Eases Overthinking

What does it look like to apply this curiosity to your stories as your mind spins with them? Well, it starts in the body. Dropping your focus from up in your mind, where the stories live, and down into your body is the first step. Simply notice the physical sensations showing up in your body. Do you feel tightness anywhere? Is your jaw clenched? Do you feel waves of heat moving through your chest or stomach?

Some can easily tune in to sensations throughout their bodies. Others find this more difficult. There were many times when I was only able to notice a tiny area of my body, like my head or a fingernail or a big toe. For some, this may be hard to understand! I was convinced something was wrong with me for a long time because I couldn't feel the rest of my body. But I've come to understand that in those moments of numbness, I'm experiencing profound fear. And it turns out that dissociating from my body was an excellent tool I learned to use in the face of intolerable fear or emotions. It allowed me to cope all those years ago during my sexual abuse experience. It enabled me to get through situations that invoked fear and anxiety, but to do so without really having to be there. So many of us learn to do this. And what a gift this skill is if trauma or unbearable emotions were part of your experience.

The good news is that when you find your mind ruminating over the stories, this tool can help bring relief, whether you can feel your body easily or not. When you realize your mind is stuck in a story spiral, drop your focus into your body and notice any present sensations, big or small. Become curious about what part of you is visiting in that moment as you notice what emotions are circling beneath your stories. Is the visiting part feeling scared, angry, sad, worried, or wrong? Is it feeling alone or not enough or afraid it will be abandoned or rejected? You see, there's a big difference between being *in* an emotion and being *with* it. When our mind focuses on the stories, this leads us to feel stuck *in* the underlying emotion. When we drop into our bodies to tune in to the emotions sitting below our stories, we're *with* our emotions. And it feels different.

Taking these micro-moment pauses to notice the underlying emotions in your body beneath your stories begins to unpin them. It creates room for them to be felt by you, even for a few seconds. When a part of us shows up with a big, uncomfortable emotion, that feeling grows louder because that part of us is trying to get our attention. And contrary to what our thinking minds believe, these parts of us are desperate to be seen and acknowledged for exactly how they're feeling. They're aching for us to be present with them while they feel this way, again, even for a few seconds if that's all that feels tolerable at the start.

It may sound scary to think of turning toward the uncomfortable feelings that sit beneath your stories. When I paused to notice the relentless, spinning stories in my mind, it quickly became obvious that the stories repeatedly worsened my stress and anxiety instead of easing them. I reluctantly tried this newer way. I'd be thirty minutes into a story-spinning session before realizing it and dropping my focus into my body. I always found underlying emotions tucked inside my body. Part of me, often young, frequently showed up expressing that feeling and freaking out. Sometimes she felt panic or shame, wrongness, not-enoughness, sadness, aloneness, anger, or resentment. The list could go on. As I acknowledged whatever feeling was there, sometimes for a few minutes and sometimes for mere seconds, something in my cells relaxed. I felt a sliver of relief that felt impossible when solely focusing on the stories in my mind.

Can you see all the ways our stories can slip into our experiences and impact how we feel as we move through them? The goal will never be to get rid of our stories. They are woven into the very essence of our human journey and can create beautiful containers of understanding for us. But it's powerful to notice what lens we are using when we form and tell a story. When a story is birthed through a lens of wrongness, it creates a sense of smallness, limited possibilities, and perspectives. It conveys black-and-white, all-or-nothing thinking about the topic at hand and convinces us our unwanted feelings, experiences or selves are undeniably wrong and need to be fixed or eliminated. But as you've seen throughout this book, applying a lens of curiosity can change the game. I invite you to notice the stories that are alive in your life. Notice how they make you feel: expansive or small, wise or wrong. Observe whether they leave you feeling a sense of possibilities or limited solutions. The best part? Simply pausing to notice how your stories make you feel automatically ushers in a lens of curiosity. And before you know it, you're on your way to embodying the truth that, in a world that makes you feel wrong, there's always been rightness within you.

Afterword

BORROWED BELIEFS

A few months before I finished writing this book, I signed up for a virtual breathwork class, which I've come to love because it quiets my ever-present thinking mind. Afterward, as I lay on my floor in a meditative state, I heard a voice say, "Honey, you don't have to carry this weight anymore. It was never yours, and you don't have to carry it." I immediately knew the voice was referring to the weight of wrongness I'd carried within me and I was stunned to understand that this belief had *never* been mine. I'd been borrowing it and didn't need to carry it as my own anymore.

A couple of nights later, I grabbed my journal to jot down a spiraling collection of concerns about the painful writer's block I'd been in for many months. I wrote a few sentences *to* the God Gang about it and asked for a response *from* them. The GG promptly reminded me: my only ten percent was to sit down and start writing. And their ninety percent was to send me the words. Well, let me tell you, this reminder was earth-shattering to my doubting mind after almost a year of painful writer's block. To hear that my job was so simple and that I didn't need to find the words because they would send them to me? Holy cow. And it turned out to be true. The stories of doubt dissolved as I consistently sat down to write from that point on and found the words flowing to me with ease once again.

This Truth Is Yours Too

It wasn't a coincidence that I had this profound experience while writing this book. I was writing a book about how it's time to discover how right you are in a world that makes you feel so wrong. And unexpectedly, I was shown that this weight of wrongness I'd carried for so long was never mine and that I didn't need to carry it anymore. And you don't need to carry it anymore either, my friend. This lens of wrongness feels like our own, but we've borrowed it from our culture, family, social circles, religion, and beyond. It beckons us to perpetually hunt for what's wrong in us or our lives and work to fix or eliminate this wrongness or brokenness, so we can finally feel worthy and start living. It reflexively creates an inner war as we fight against those emotions and experiences like anxiety, grief, anger, confusion, sore throat, migraine, chronic illness, and even cancer.

My hope is that this book shows you how possible it is to form an updated relationship with yourself and all the different parts of you, so it becomes easier to see the wisdom and wholeness that have been yours all along. May this book leave you feeling hope as you navigate all the seeming wrongness in your life. May you understand that it will *never* be necessary for you to use any of the mentioned tools in a perfect way to experience their benefit. May you know that you never needed to be a relentless self-improvement project to finally earn your worth because your worth has been intricately woven into your very existence since before you took your first breath. May you realize you will never need to pause and come back home to yourself in *every* micro-moment for those intermittent pauses to be powerful in your life. May you continue on this journey understanding that curiosity is a true antidote to the lens of wrongness that's owned so many of us for too long and that incredible rightness has been woven inside your seeming wrongness all along. I hope this book shows you how to end the exhaustion and find you are utterly wise, mighty, held, and whole. It's time for you to discover how right you are in a world that makes you feel so wrong.

ACKNOWLEDGMENTS

My plan to write this book began twenty-three years ago in Boston, Massachusetts. The birthing of this book obviously took some time, but that's a funny thing about dreams. Sometimes, they need to cook for a long while before they're ready to be dusted off and have new life breathed into them.

Many beloved people have supported me as I've grown and unfolded into the version of me that was ready to live into my book-writing endeavors.

Tammy Letherer, Ronaldo Alves, Kevin Stone, Alex Kale, Kyle McCord, Cameron Finch, and Atmosphere Press, when I thought I'd finished growing through this writing experience, you invited me to stretch more, and I am so glad I did. Thank you for supporting me in creating this final version of my beloved book and for helping it reach the world.

Carolyn Flynn, you are a gift to me. You repeatedly sliced through my confusion and guided me to clarity and inner knowing. You saw the big picture before I could. You believed in me and lovingly shepherded me through the many stages of this book, including painful writer's block. I am forever grateful to you for sharing your talents with me. And I thank KN Literary for introducing us.

Talking Book Studio, thank you for landing yourselves in my backyard mountains of WNC! Recording my audiobook with y'all (whoa, I sound southern!) became an empowering and unexpectedly fun adventure!

Kelly Hoogenakker, Lauren Milling, Connie Burns, Dad, Leslie, Laura Linde, Kathy Kestle, and Shanon Sidell, thank you for being beta readers. The insight and feedback you each offered in the various iterations of this book were invaluable to me.

Lisa Listerman, Monica Scamardo, Shannon Sandrea, Kelly Hoogenakker, Laura Linde, Karen Hurley, Lori Starn, Caity Donahoe, Shannon Sidell, Melody Lyman, Janell Cooper, Radha Hamilton, John Hoogenakker, and Chris Petrie, thank you for the unique ways you each supported, celebrated, and contributed to my journey in writing and publishing *What If You're Right?*. I'm forever grateful for the myriad instances you showed up when I needed to bounce ideas, sections of text, angst, title possibilities, or even book covers off you.

Leslie, you are my person. You have believed in me endlessly, even when I couldn't. And you have always championed my dreams, including this one. Thank you for opening me to faces of love I never dared to know until you.

Winslow and Serette, I envisioned many things when I came to be your mom, but your genuine support and interest in my journey as an author have been unexpected and utterly heart-filling. I learn more from you every day about what it means to love.

Dad, thank you for your ever-present openness to understanding my perspectives and experiences, your bottomless support, and for infusing me with your gift of writing.

Mom, thank you for imbuing me with your passion for the emotional journey of all humans and for cheering me on since the inception of this book and sharing its ideas with others far before it was published!

Sanna, what a journey! Thank you for being here for all of it, for understanding in ways no one else can, believing in me, and finding me funny!

Mand, even though your support was in wordless form during this particular passage of time, I frequently envisioned your appreciation of specific phrases or chapters as this book came to life.

Connie, thank you for helping me discover parts of me that I never knew existed. And for walking alongside me and guiding me as I uncovered so many gifts tucked inside the seeming wrongness of these parts. You have been pivotal in my unfolding into this version of who I am today. I love this version of me so much, and I love you.

Donna Wetterstrand, you first gave me words for my "whale of wrongness," which changed my life. I'm more grateful than you'll ever know.

Hackley School and Mr. Naething, thank you for helping me cultivate writing skills that continue to influence me today.

My treasured patients, you may never know how much you have each taught me over the last thirty-plus years. Thank you for inviting me to be a part of your journey, whether for a moment, a season, or longer and for trusting me with the sacredness of your mind, body, emotions, and soul.

Lastly, I thank my God Gang for traveling this path with me and reminding me that I simply needed to sit down and start writing, and they would send me the words.

Dr. Colwell's Micro-Moment Reset Audio:

Scan this QR code to access and download the audio.
It can also be accessed here:
www.dremilycolwell.com/free-gift.

ABOUT THE AUTHOR

DR. EMILY COLWELL is a licensed and board-certified naturopathic doctor and clinical social worker whose extensive career spans three decades. Her academic journey took her from Columbia University's School of Social Work, where she earned a master's degree, to Bastyr University in Seattle, where she earned her doctorate in naturopathic medicine in 2006. She continues to blend her expertise in clinical social work and naturopathic medicine into her current practice, where she addresses the emotional health of patients, as she finds this has a profound and lasting impact on physical health as well.

Emily's personal encounters with anxiety, childhood trauma, family addiction, chronic illness, shifting sexual orientation, and cancer have been her teachers, showing her the capacity for healing, regardless of the circumstances.

These days, Emily dabbles in comical antics, group karaoke, and morning squats. She invites you to visit her at www.dremilycolwell.com or follow her on Instagram @dr.emily_colwell or Facebook @emilycolwell.naturopathic physician.5.

ABOUT ATMOSPHERE PRESS

Founded in 2015, Atmosphere Press was built on the principles of Honesty, Transparency, Professionalism, Kindness, and Making Your Book Awesome. As an ethical and author-friendly hybrid press, we stay true to that founding mission today.

If you're a reader, enter our giveaway for a free book here:

SCAN TO ENTER
BOOK GIVEAWAY

If you're a writer, submit your manuscript for consideration here:

SCAN TO SUBMIT
MANUSCRIPT

And always feel free to visit Atmosphere Press and our authors online at atmospherepress.com. See you there soon!